STEP · BY · STEP
JAPANESE COOKING

LESLEY DOWNER AND MINORU YONEDA

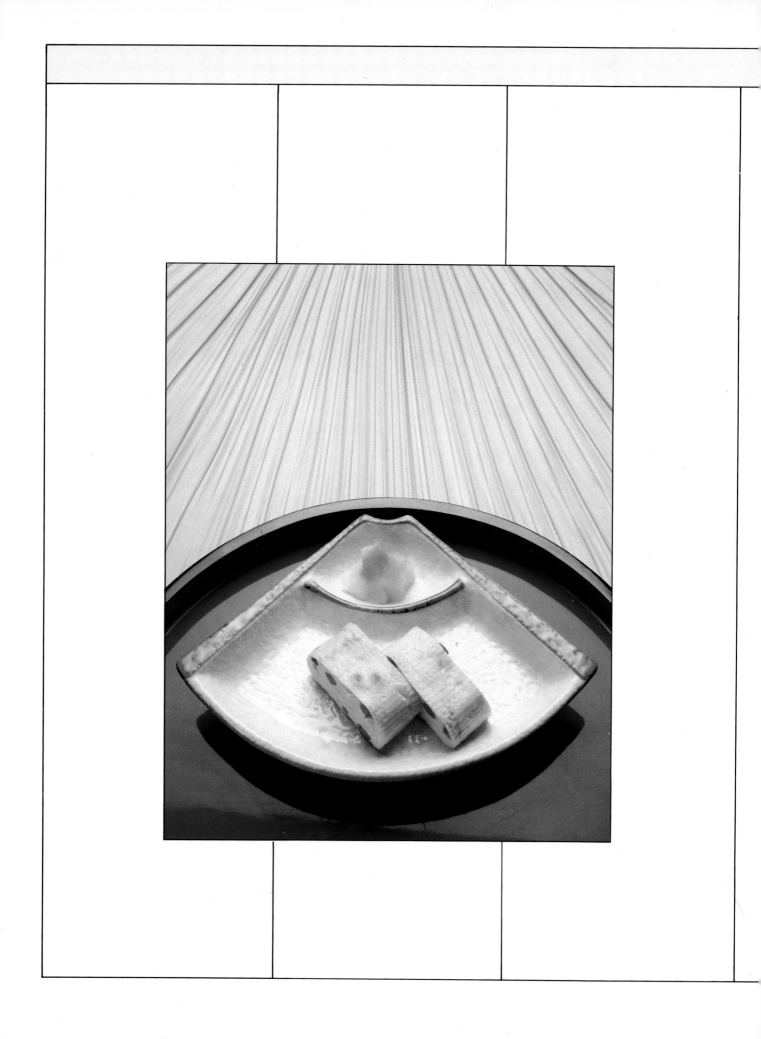

STEP · BY · STEP
JAPANESE COOKING

LESLEY DOWNER AND MINORU YONEDA

BARRON'S

Woodbury, New York • Toronto

A QUARTO BOOK

First U.S. and Canadian edition published
1986 by Barron's Educational Series, Inc.

Copyright © Quarto Publishing Ltd

All inquiries should be addressed to:
Barron's Educational Series, Inc.
113 Crossways Park Drive
Woodbury, New York 11797

International Standard Book No. 0-8120-5688-4

Library of Congress Catalog
Card No.: 85-30617

6789 987654321

This book was designed and produced by
Quarto Publishing Ltd
The Old Brewery, 6 Blundell Street
London N7 9BH

Senior Editor: Stephen Paul
Editor: Susie Ward

Desiger: Pete Laws
Art Editor: Moria Clinch

Photographer: John Hesletine

Art Director: Alastair Campbell
Editorial Director: Jim Miles

Typeset by Facsimile Graphics Ltd
    Coggeshall, Essex
Color origination by Rainbow Graphic Arts
    Co Ltd, Hong Kong
Printed by Lee Fung Asco Printers Ltd,
    Hong Kong

Quarto Publishing would like to take this
opportunity to thank the Restaurant Yamato
for all their kind help and assistance in the
production of this book. Without their
generous support and the dedication of the
owner, Charles Cosham, the book would not
have been possible.

Contents

Foreword

As a Japanese chef working abroad I have been delighted by the increasing popularity of Japanese food among Westerners. Indeed, in many Japanese restaurants the majority of the diners are now Westerners whereas only a few years ago these same restaurants were patronized almost entirely by Japanese tourists.

Reflecting this boom a number of books on Japanese cooking have appeared — some are quite good but most seem to endorse the widespread myth that Japanese cooking is very difficult and time consuming.

Many of my Western friends, having experienced Japanese food in restaurants, have sought my advice on how to prepare it at home. This has not always been easy since circumstances in the West are very different to those in Japan, and to prepare authentic Japanese food requires a fair amount of experimentation and improvisation.

When I was invited to participate in this book I knew immediately what an ambitious project it was, but I also knew that the timing was just right. When I met my co-author, Lesley Downer, who impressed me greatly with her thorough knowledge of Japan and Japanese food, I realized that the project was a golden opportunity to share with people all over the world the joys of cooking and eating Japanese food.

As with all human works, mistakes are inevitable, especially in difficult circumstances, but these mistakes can be corrected as time goes by and the work constantly improved. I have tried to present authentic traditional Japanese cooking that can be prepared at home, but I am open to criticism and indeed I believe that it won't be long before Western chefs can cook Japanese food better than Japanese chefs.

MINORU YONEDA

INTRODUCTION

Every spring in Japan there comes a day when all the newspaper headlines carry the news that today the cherry blossoms are at their peak. The precise day that this occurs moves like a wave through Japan from south to north. On the eagerly-awaited day, many a toiling office worker downs tools and sets out to admire the pink blossoms and to feast and quaff sake beneath them.

The attraction of the cherry blossoms, striking a chord in every Japanese heart, is their transience. Even as the revellers eat and sing, the cherry blossoms are already fading, and soon begin to float downwards like pink snow. Our Western cherry blossoms, which linger on for two or three weeks, are most disappointing to the Japanese visitor.

The Japanese have always appreciated the beauty of the ephemeral. What could be more ephemeral than food, produced only to be immediately eaten? Yet the Japanese chef feels it well worth his while to turn every meal he creates into a work of art.

On first seeing a formal Japanese meal, one hardly dares to disturb the perfection of the tiny morsels of food arranged to form exquisite designs on the plates and bowls which form the background. The Japanese themselves tend to be more interested in the visual qualities of the meal before them than in its taste. A meal in the best restaurant in Tokyo may well taste heavenly, but what will most excite the admiration of the Japanese diner will be the way in which the chef has transformed simple vegetables, fish and meat into an edible masterpiece.

This concern with the visual quality of the meal is not the preserve of restaurants. A simple home-cooked meal will consist — not of a heaping plateful of food as in the West — but of tiny portions of various foods, selected as much for their variety of form, shape and color, as for their taste. They are always neatly arranged with an eye to their appearance and carefully garnished with tiny sprigs of green or a delicate scatter of poppy seeds.

There are several levels to the design of a Japanese meal. Each individual item of food is carefully prepared to enhance its visual qualities. Lowly vegetables may be used as decorative garnish, be it a carrot cherry blossom or a turnip chrysanthemum. The prepared foods are then artistically arranged on small plates, sometimes forming a miniature landscape. The plates and serving dishes are laid out on the lacquered trays according to prescribed rules. The setting is one of harmony and stillness.

In the West we are relatively functional in our approach to food. We eat when we are hungry, to sustain our bodies. We plan a meal in terms of taste and nutritional content, vitamins, minerals and carbohydrates. In Japan food has perhaps a wider significance than in the West. It is not just to fill the stomach and keep the body working: it has an aesthetic, ritual and social role to play too.

Nowhere is this more apparent than in the tea ceremony, where the actual drinking of the bitter green tea is incidental. The essence of the ceremony lies in the perfection, the economy and precision, of each gesture involved in the making and drinking of the tea.

Fortunately for Western cooks, it is primarily the aesthetic element in Japanese cuisine which makes it seem difficult. Cooking methods are deliberately simple, designed to remain as faithful as possible to the original ingredients, rather than transforming them into something unrecognizable, concealed by spices or drowned by heavy masking sauces.

The Japanese have a deep-rooted respect for nature, shown in their annual pilgrimages to admire the cherry blossoms, and they express their love of nature in their treatment of their daily food. Japanese cooking relies on the quality of the ingredients, which must therefore be of the finest, and absolutely fresh. Early every morning Tokyo chefs visit the great Tsukiji market to seek out the

ABOVE *Kyoto, the cultural capital of Japan, is famous for its Zen-inspired temple cuisine.*

freshest meat, fish and vegetables for the day's cooking. Housewives too shop every day, throwing away food which has become even a little tired. Half the art of Japanese cuisine lies in the ability to select the finest ingredients.

The freshest and highest-quality ingredients, usually fish — though sometimes beef, vegetables and *tofu* — are served uncooked, just as they are, as *sashimi.* For *sashimi,* clearly only the best and freshest fish will do. Tokyoites make special journeys to small towns along the coast to eat fish straight from the sea. And if you visit one of Tokyo's best *sashimi* restaurants, you may be invited to select your fish from the aquarium, to be netted and spirited into the kitchens. Within a few minutes it reappears neatly sliced on your table.

Japanese comestibles change with the seasons, so that it is always appropriately seasonal produce which is served. But Japanese sensitivity to the passing of the seasons extends beyond this. The appearance of the cherry blossom signifies the coming of spring, an event to be celebrated with almost pagan rapture. Not only are tables laden with the fish and vegetables of spring; cherry blossoms appear everywhere, even in tea.

Tradition governs the food and cooking which are considered suitable to each season. As the year passes, so the menu changes, to reflect and to remind us of the passing seasons. On the first day of spring, people discard their heavy winter clothes no matter what the actual weather, and the thick warming stews of winter are replaced by more delicate dishes to show off the season's fresh young vegetables and fish. The steamy days of summer are made more bearable by chilled dishes served on a bed of ice cubes. And the chestnuts and wild mushrooms of fall may be served on a red and gold leaf instead of a plate.

The range of fruit, vegetables and meat in Japan is limited, not only by the season, but also by the land itself. Japan is made up of a group of small crowded islands. Half of

the land area consists of steep, heavily-wooden mountains, usable neither for building nor cultivation. Every inch of the remaining land is put to use. Much of the land not occupied by buildings is used for rice cultivation. Green paddy fields in neat oblongs stretch across much of the flat plain of Central Japan. Even in Tokyo suburbs old ladies can be seen planting out the tiny rice shoots in spring in small paddy fields overshadowed by skyscrapers. There is no equivalent in Western cooking to the dominance of rice. Rice is more than just a staple; it is food itself, designated by the same word, *gohan*. Most Japanese eat rice

three times a day and consider all other dishes as accompaniment whose purpose is merely to whet the appetite for the real food, the rice.

Those areas unsuitable for rice cultivation are given over to vegetables, and Japanese markets are always full of a huge variety of vegetables, invariably glistening fresh and quite perfect in shape as well as quality. Taking advantage of every spare inch, the Japanese also comb the river banks and field borders for wild vegetables in the spring. In the fall, the densely wooded mountains are thick with mushroom hunters.

FAR LEFT *Cherry blossoms (top) in Kyoto. On the day the blossoms peak the whole of Japan pauses to admire their transient beauty. With cultivable land at a premium, even the foothills of Mount Fuji (bottom) bear crops.* ABOVE *Macha is the tea used for the fascinating tea ceremony, a ceremony that is structured around a complex etiquette.*

There is no space in Japan for animals to be kept in any quantity. On the central island of Honshu, apart from the odd cow living, rather incongruously, in a tiny shed beside the railway track of the main line out of Tokyo into the suburbs, there are no animals to be seen. In Kobe, beef cattle are said to be reared underground, where they live an extremely pampered though somewhat short life, enjoying a rich diet and daily massage to produce what some say is the finest beef in the world. Until the opening of Japan to the West at the end of the last century, the Japanese did not eat meat, although chicken has always been a part of the Japanese diet. Even today meat is not eaten in Japan nearly as frequently as it is in the West; milk and milk products also tend to be used less.

Since the earliest times, venturing beyond the limitations of the land, the Japanese have made the harvest of the sea an essential part of their diet. Rather like England, no part of the many islands that make up Japan is very far from water; the rivers and seas are full of an abundance, not only of fish, but of seafoods and seaweeds, which are harvested with thoroughness and ingenuity. The variety and quality of fish and seafoods available in Japan is quite unparalleled. It is foods from the sea which dominate the Japanese menu.

Perhaps through the influence of Zen, the Japanese taste tends towards the ascetic. In cookery, the emphasis is on exceptional quality simply served, rather than on complexity of cooking method or spicing. Foods tend to be served separately rather than in combination, so that each individual taste can be fully appreciated. Flavoring is minimal. The essential flavorings of Japanese cooking are only two, *dashi*, the basic stock for soups and simmerings, made from kelp (*kombu*) and dried bonito flakes, and soy sauce. The highlight of a Japanese meal is *sashimi*, superlatively fresh uncooked fish, expertly sliced. The art of cutting is surrounded with mystique. It is said to take at least 10

years to qualify as a *sashimi* chef, and most housewives would not venture to cut their own *sashimi* or indeed the beef for *sukiyaki*, but buy it ready-sliced.

As with so many aspects of Japanese life, cooking techniques are neatly categorized. A Japanese meal is planned around a balance of techniques rather than nutritional considerations. A formal meal, such as one would eat in a restaurant or at a banquet, consists of a succession of dishes: first a clear soup, then a raw fish dish, followed by a simmered dish, a grilled dish, a deep-fried dish, a steamed dish and a dressed salad. A simpler home cooked meal is made up of a selection of dishes cooked using different techniques. In either case, the meal ends with the real food, rice, together with some crunchy pickles and probably a bowl of thick soup made from *miso*, a salty fermented soy bean paste.

Japan is a long, narrow country whose various regions have dramatically contrasting climates. Travelling north by train from the relatively warm streets of Tokyo, one can find oneself within an hour walled

in by snow. Kyushu in the south is nearly tropical, whereas northern Hokkaido has a climate and landscape very similar to England. Each region has its typical range of produce, and different traditions of cookery have arisen in response to each local environment. The northerners, with their long cold winters, like to gather together cosily to cook warming one-pot dishes and stews at the table, while Tokyo dwellers combat their humid summers with a tasty dish of eel. Each small town has its speciality, be it salmon from Hokkaido, oysters from Hiroshima, or *miso* from Takayama in the mountains of Central Japan, and has developed characteristic methods of cooking it. Japanese cooking ranges also from the exquisite morsels of the Zen-inspired temple cuisine of Kyoto, the cultural capital of Japan, to the hearty home cooked dishes of the countryside.

Such variations only serve to emphasize the common thread that runs through all these manifestations of Japanese cuisine, rooted as it is in the age-old Japanese response to nature and to the countryside.

FAR LEFT *Half of Japan's total cultivable area is given over to the rice crop, much of which is grown in terraced paddy fields.* ABOVE *Choice of the finest and freshest ingredients is absolutely fundamental to Japanese cooking, and fish markets are visited on a daily basis by restaurant chefs and housewives alike.*

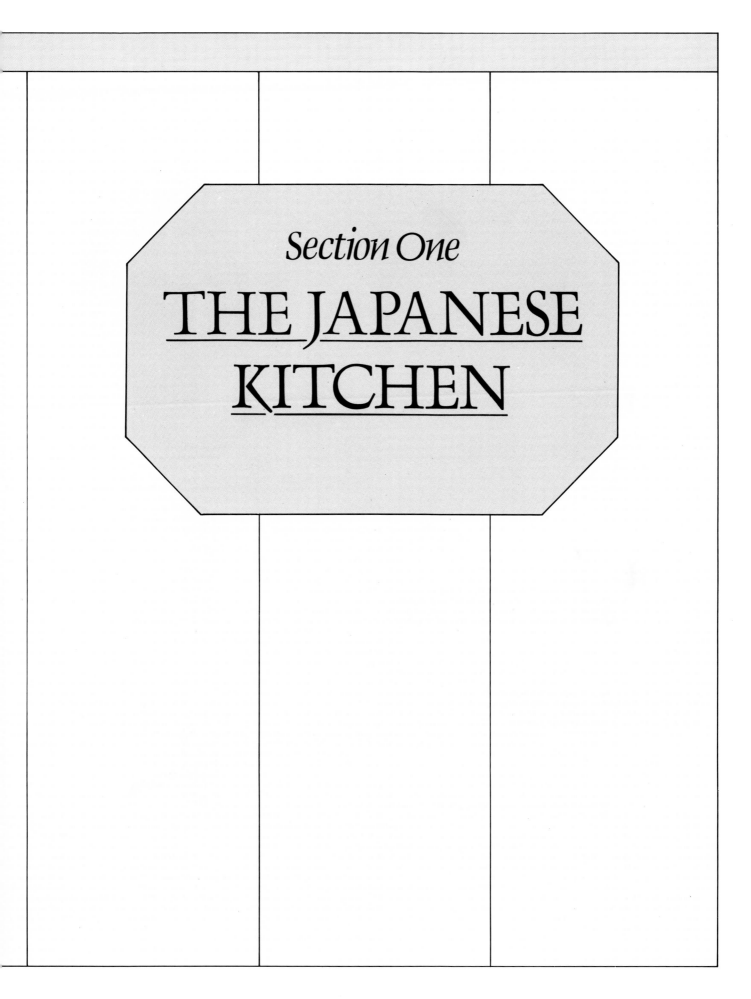

Section One

THE JAPANESE KITCHEN

UTENSILS

Japanese meals may be successfully prepared using utensils available in any well equipped Western kitchen, with just a little improvisation. In fact most Japanese kitchens are cramped and somewhat less complete and convenient than the average Western kitchen. However, with their characteristic love of precision and the right tool for each task, the Japanese have developed a range of kitchen utensils which, although not essential, are very useful in preparing Japanese dishes. They also make an aesthetically pleasing addition to the kitchen. The following utensils are available in Oriental stores and are, in general, inexpensive and long lasting.

It is not essential to use Japanese knives, but you should have several good sharp knives which perform the same functions. Japanese knives are made of carbon steel, and are always honed on a whetstone.

ABOVE *Both metal and bamboo steamers (*mushiki*) are used in Japan. Stacking bamboo steamers are readily available in Chinese stores and are most efficient. Bamboo makes a better insulator than metal, ensuring that more heat is retained.*

Steamers may be simply improvised. Use a large covered saucepan containing some support to keep the cooking vessels above the level of the water. A cloth stretched under the lid will absorb excess moisture.

TOP *This vegetable knife (*nakiri-bocho*) performs all manner of delicate vegetable cutting operations — from chopping and slicing to fine paring — with efficiency and speed. It has no Western equivalent, and is a worthwhile investment.*

CENTER *This long thin-bladed* sashimi *knife (*sashimi-bocho*) is used for cutting fish fillets. A Western meat slicer may be used instead.*

BOTTOM *A basic kitchen knife is used for both general fish and meat cutting and also for more delicate work. It is available in many sizes.*

LEFT *A fine-meshed strainer is used for draining noodles.* BELOW *A small round frying-pan (*oyako-nabe*) is sometimes used for making omelets.*

BELOW *A cast iron* sukiyaki *pan (*sukiyaki-nabe*) is traditionally used to cook* sukiyaki *at table. A deep heavy frying-pan may be used as a substitute. Like any cast iron pan, a* sukiyaki *pan should be seasoned before use and wiped clean or washed without detergent.*

ABOVE *Japanese omelets are made in a small rectangular omelet pan (*makiyaki-nabe*) to make a neat oblong which is rolled as it is fried.*

BELOW *A drop lid (*otochi-buta*) made of cypress or cedar with a small handle is used for simmering. It floats on the simmering stock, ensuring that the foods are completely submerged and cook evenly, preventing them from being tossed around. The drop lid should always be moistened before use. These lids are sold in Japanese stores: a flat light lid or bamboo plate is a possible substitute, as is a circle of waxed paper.*

RIGHT *A small flexible bamboo mat is used for making sushi. Sushi may be rolled by hand, but will be less firmly and evenly packed.*

ABOVE *A small flat bamboo rice paddle is used to turn and fluff cooked rice, and to mix seasonings into sushi rice. A flat wooden spoon may be used as a substitute.*

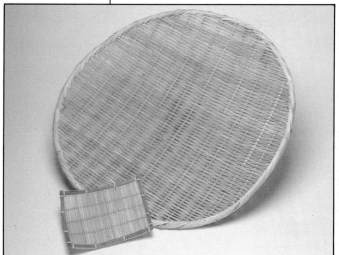

ABOVE *The Japanese mortar and pestle (suribachi and surikogi) is a beautiful utensil as well as being extremely efficient. The mortar is a heavy ceramic bowl, serrated on the inside, in which foods such as nuts and sesame seeds are ground with a large wooden pestle.*

ABOVE *A bamboo strainer (zaru) is the traditional utensil for straining and draining food.*

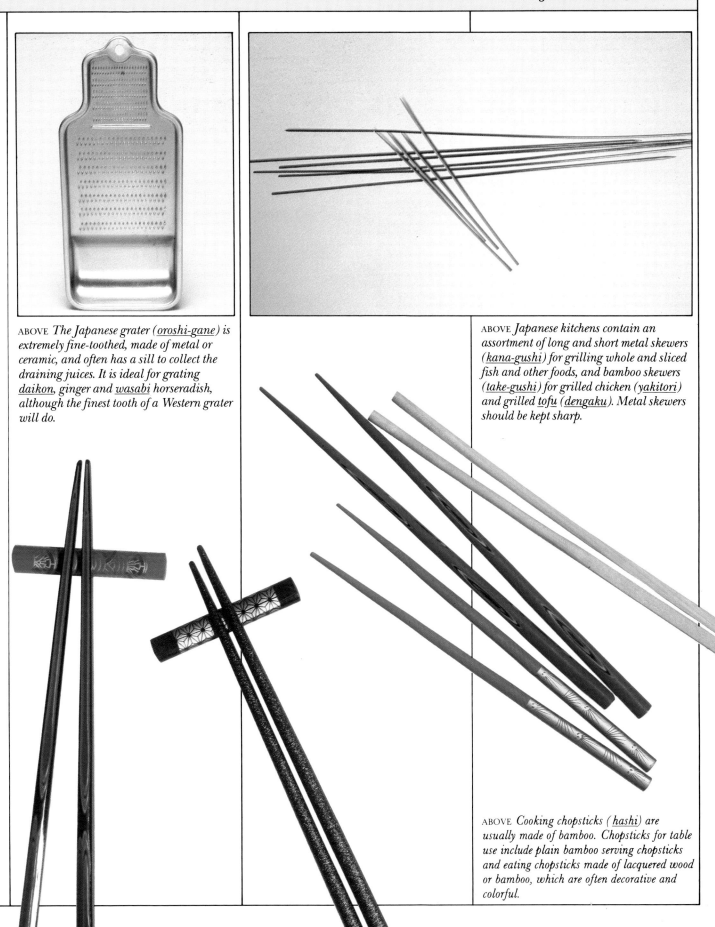

ABOVE *The Japanese grater (<u>oroshi-gane</u>) is extremely fine-toothed, made of metal or ceramic, and often has a sill to collect the draining juices. It is ideal for grating <u>daikon</u>, ginger and <u>wasabi</u> horseradish, although the finest tooth of a Western grater will do.*

ABOVE *Japanese kitchens contain an assortment of long and short metal skewers (<u>kana-gushi</u>) for grilling whole and sliced fish and other foods, and bamboo skewers (<u>take-gushi</u>) for grilled chicken (<u>yakitori</u>) and grilled <u>tofu</u> (<u>dengaku</u>). Metal skewers should be kept sharp.*

ABOVE *Cooking chopsticks (<u>hashi</u>) are usually made of bamboo. Chopsticks for table use include plain bamboo serving chopsticks and eating chopsticks made of lacquered wood or bamboo, which are often decorative and colorful.*

RIGHT *One-pot dishes are traditionally made in a heavy lidded earthenware casserole, which is ideal for the purpose. An even distributor of heat, it can be placed over a direct flame if the outside surface is completely dry. It also looks very attractive on the table. An ovenproof ceramic casserole is a good substitute.*

BELOW *Every Japanese kitchen contains a variety of fine tableware, including lacquered wooden bowls with domed lids for soup; tall lidded cups for savory steamed custard (chawan mushi); delicate porcelain bowls for rice; and small flat dishes for pickles.*

LEFT *Japanese tableware is often very fine, and some items may be heirlooms. Deep bowls are used for delicate or soft foods. Dishes accompanied by sauces may be served on porcelain plates with a special compartment for the sauce, in a variety of attractive shapes.*

BELOW *A Japanese teacup and pot; and a* sake *flask and appropriate cup.*

INGREDIENTS

The cooking methods of Japanese cuisine are deliberately simple, so that the focus is centered firmly on the ingredients. These may be visually transformed through cutting, but their flavor remains as unadulterated as possible. The most important stage in the preparation of a Japanese meal is the selection of the vegetables, meats, fish or fruit to be used, and to obtain an authentic Japanese taste it is essential to use authentic ingredients.

However, we must also take into account the *spirit* of Japanese cuisine, which requires every ingredient to be of the best quality and absolutely fresh. In effect, this means that the ingredients must be of the season and of the locality. Therefore, for the Westerner to cook with seasonal and locally available fish and vegetables is to remain very much within the spirit of Japanese cuisine. Some staples, like soy sauce, are widely available, while others may be found only in oriental or specifically Japanese food stores (you will find a list of Japanese food stores in the back of this book). In the following pages we suggest substitutes for those ingredients which may be difficult to obtain, in the hope that although the flavor may not be absolutely authentic, the dish may be prepared in the spirit of Japanese cuisine.

Some essential Japanese ingredients

The following are some of the basic ingredients to be found in every Japanese kitchen:

Dashi
Dashi, made from dried bonito flakes and kelp *(kombu),* is the basic stock of the Japanese kitchen. It is *dashi* which is responsible for giving the characteristic Japanese flavor to many dishes, and the ability to make well flavored *dashi* is the essential secret of the good cook. Today various types of instant *dashi* are sold under the name *dashi-no-moto,* and some are very good, as well as quick and convenient to use. Instant *dashi* is available in Japanese and some Chinese food stores.

Ginger
Fresh ginger root is much used in Japanese cookery as a seasoning and garnish; it is widely available, particularly in shops specializing in oriental or African foods. Dried ginger is not a substitute. To use, peel the skin of the required amount before grating.

Squeeze freshly grated ginger to obtain ginger juice.

Sweet pickled ginger *(beni-shoga)* is always served as a garnish with *sushi.* Long red ginger shoots *(hajikami shoga)* make a decorative and piquant garnish for grilled foods, particularly grilled fish.

Fish cake (Kamaboko)
Kamaboko is made from pureed white fish, pressed into solid cakes and sold ready cooked; it is usually white or tinted pink. It can be simply sliced and eaten raw, and is a popular ingredient in one-pot dishes, soups and rice and noodle

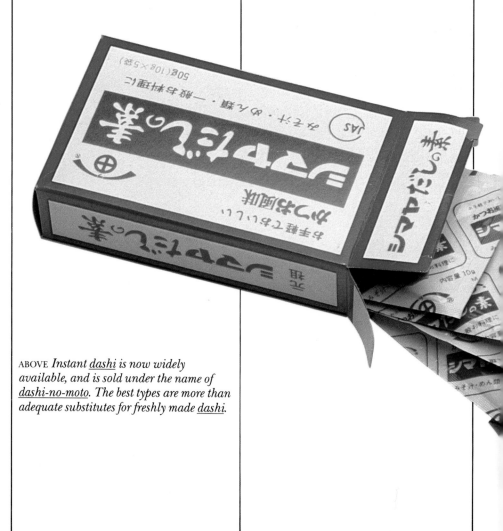

ABOVE *Instant dashi is now widely available, and is sold under the name of dashi-no-moto. The best types are more than adequate substitutes for freshly made dashi.*

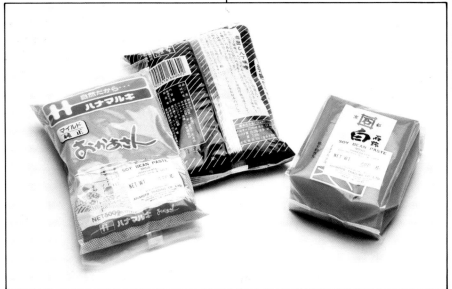

dishes. *Kamaboko* is widely available in Japanese food stores; it should be stored in the refrigerator.

Horseradish *(Wasabi)*

Horseradish is rather a misnomer for *wasabi*, the grated root of a riverside plant native to Japan. In *sushi* bar parlance *wasabi* is known as *namida,* "tears", for it brings tears to the eyes. It is sold in Japanese food stores ready made in tubes, and in powder form, to be mixed up as required with a little water to a smooth paste. *Wasabi* is the usual accompaniment for raw fish dishes.

Kinome

Kinome, the fresh-tasting young leaves of the prickly ash, is the most widely used garnish in Japan. Tiny sprigs of parsley or watercress may be used as a substitute touch of green, although the taste is completely different.

Kuzu

Kuzu is produced from the root of the *kuzu* vine, and is a traditional Japanese thickener which gives a particular light and translucent quality to sauces and soups; it is also used to give a crisp coating to fried foods. It is reputed in Japan for its medicinal properties. *Kuzu* is sold in Japanese stores and health food stores, but is expensive. Cornstarch or arrowroot are acceptable substitutes.

Mirin

Mirin, a sweet golden cooking wine with a very low alcohol content, is an essential item in the Japanese kitchen, giving a distinctive mild sweetness to simmering liquids, glazes and dipping sauces. It is available in Japanese food stores everywhere. If unobtainable, simply use a little sugar (1 tsp for 1 Tbsp *mirin*), as a substitute.

Miso

Miso is a rich and savory paste produced by the fermenting action of a yeast-like mold on cooked soybeans, which are often mixed with rice or other grains. It takes at least six months and as much as three years to mature. *Miso* is a peculiarly Japanese food; indeed, as *miso*

ABOVE LEFT *Pickled long red ginger shoots (hajikami shoga) are useful for garnishing grilled foods, especially grilled fish.*
ABOVE *Miso is also available from shops ready packaged. The white version is used for sauces and light miso soups, and the red miso is used for rich soups and for general cooking purposes.*

soup, it is probably eaten by every Japanese every day. It is much used in Japanese cooking as a basic flavoring, as a dressing for simmered and grilled foods and even as a pickling medium. There are many different varieties and colors of *miso*; basically the lighter white version is used for sauces and light *miso* soups, while the thicker red miso is used for richer soups and for general cooking purposes. *Miso* is available in health food stores as well as Japanese stores. An extremely nutritious food containing living enzymes, it should be kept under refrigeration.

Noodles

Noodles are one of the most popular Japanese foods and come in many varieties and sizes. Broad white wheat noodles, *udon,* are particularly associated with Osaka and Southern Japan. Brown buckwheat noodles, *soba,* are popular in Tokyo and Northern Japan. *Chasoba* is a variety of *soba* made with green tea. *Harusame,* which romantically translates as "spring rain", are very fine translucent white noodles made from rice or potato flour.

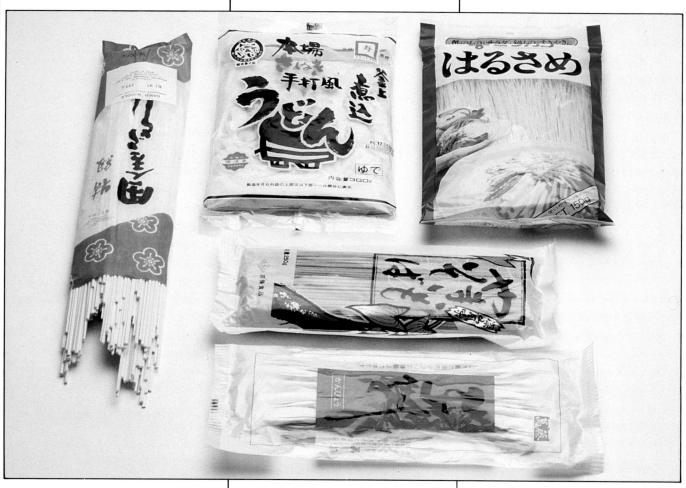

ABOVE *Noodles play a large role in the everyday Japanese diet. Most types are sold in Japanese food stores, the most popular being* udon, soba *and* harusame. RIGHT *Both* mirin *and* ponzu *sauce can be bought ready-made in bottles.*

Oils

The Japanese use pure vegetable oil, never animal fats, for cooking; any vegetable oil except olive oil is suitable. Sesame oil is prized for its delicate nutty flavor, and may be added in small amounts to the oil for deep frying. Sesame oil is available in Chinese as well as Japanese grocery stores.

Pickles *(Tsukemono)*

No Japanese meal is complete without a dish of thinly sliced pickles of various types, colors and shapes. Pickles are made from many different vegetables; the most popular include *daikon* radish, eggplant, Chinese cabbage and *shiso* buds. Nowadays pickles are usually store-bought. A selection of pickles is available in every Japanese food store. Buy several varieties and arrange a few slices on each plate.

Rice cake *(Mochi)*

Rice cakes are made by pounding glutinous rice, traditionally in big tubs, to produce a chewy white cake, which is

shaped into balls or squares.

Commercially produced rice cakes are sold in Japanese food stores. They may be simply grilled and eaten with soy sauce. Rice cakes are an essential ingredient in *ozoni*, a thick vegetable soup eaten particularly at New Year.

Sesame seeds
Sesame seeds are a characteristic Japanese flavoring and garnish. They should be lightly roasted in a dry pan to bring out the nutty flavor before use. They may then be used whole as a garnish, or lightly ground in a mortar and pestle for use in sauces and dressings. White sesame seeds are available in most oriental stores, and black — which have a slightly stronger flavor — in Japanese food stores.

Seven spice pepper (*Shichimi*)
Seven spice pepper is a grainy mixture of chili pepper, black pepper, dried orange peel, sesame seeds, poppy seeds, slivers of *nori* seaweed, and hemp seeds; the exact blend of spices varies. It is available

TOP *Packaged foodstuffs make cooking Japanese food in the West less problematical. Rice cakes, arum root (konnyaku), fish cakes (kamabuko), potato flour (katakuri) and sweet potato chips (satoimu) are all available from Japanese food stores.* ABOVE *Instant pickle powder is an acceptable substitute for home-made pickles.*

in Japanese food stores, and is used as a seasoning for cooking and as a condiment.

Soy sauce

Soy sauce, a fermentation of soybeans, wheat and salt, is one of the primary seasonings of Japanese cooking. The thinner, lighter Japanese soy sauce, of which the most well known brand is Kikkoman, should be used in preference to Chinese. The soy sauce used for general cooking purposes is dark in color, and a rather saltier, light colored variety is used to avoid darkening a light colored dish.

Soy bean curd (Tofu)

Tofu is one of the most common ingredients in Japanese cooking, used in a wide variety of dishes. It has a delicate, slightly nutty, flavor and is an easily digestible source of vegetable protein. It is made by coagulating soya milk in a process very similar to the making of cottage cheese. The best *tofu* is made fresh every day and is sold in large blocks in Chinese supermarkets and Japanese stores. Various types of long-life *tofu* are also available, as are packs of instant *tofu* mix.

Stored in the refrigerator under water, with the water changed every day, *tofu* will keep for five to six days.

Tofu is the basis for many other products. *Aburage,* golden deep-fried cakes of *tofu,* are available frozen in Japanese stores.

Vinegar

Japanese rice vinegar has a light, delicate flavor. It is available in delicatessens as well as Japanese and Chinese food stores. If unobtainable, diluted cider vinegar is an acceptable substitute. Special *sushi* vinegar is used for making *sushi.*

Yuzu

Yuzu is a tiny citrus fruit with a distinctively flavored rind, much prized as a garnish and flavoring. It is sold frozen in Japanese food stores. Lemon peel may be used as a substitute.

TOP *Dark soy sauce (left) is used for general cooking purposes, while the lighter variety (right) is used where coloring is not required.* ABOVE *Japanese rice vinegar (left) should be used when available, but diluted cider vinegar may be substituted.* Sushi *should always be made with special* sushi *vinegar (right).*

TOP *(clockwise) Ginger paste;* wasabi *paste; chili and* sancho *spices;* wasabi *powder; and monosodium glutamate.* ABOVE Shirataki *nodles, made from* konnyaku, *are widely used in one-pot dishes.*

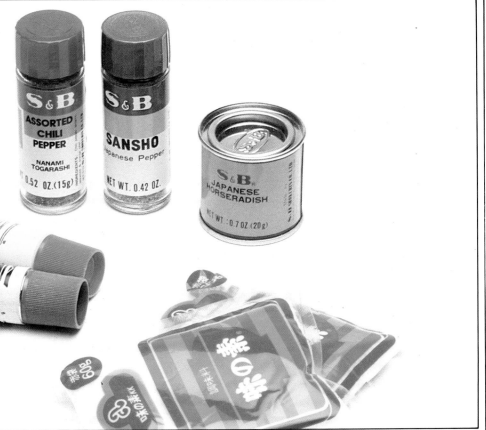

ABOVE *Sake is the national alcoholic drink of Japan and is the most suitable accompaniment to a Japanese meal.*

ABOVE *There is a wide range of long-life tofu most of which is sold in packs of instant tofu mix.*

ABOVE *Sesame oil has a delicate nutty flavor, and is sometimes added (in small quantities) to the oil for deep frying. Sesame seeds are a characteristic Japanese flavoring and garnish. The black seeds have a slightly stronger flavor.*

FOOD FROM THE SEA

Foods harvested from the sea and from Japan's many rivers play a central part in Japanese cooking. Seaweeds, both fresh and dried, hold the key to some essential Japanese flavors. And no meal would be complete without at least one fish dish. An enormous variety of fish appear on the Japanese table, varying according to the seasons and the locality. The range of fish available in the West is different from that available in Japan, so that it is always necessary to make substitutions. However, we can be sure that our cookery is within the spirit of Japanese cuisine if the fish we select are the freshest possible, and are both seasonal and local.

The Japanese eat a wide variety of fresh fish, most of which are not available in the West. It is therefore necessary to substitute within the basic categories of salt and freshwater fish, and round and flat fish, bearing in mind the basic criterion of using seasonal fish which are absolutely fresh.

The Japanese assess the freshness of a fish by the length of time it has been dead. The freshest fish come almost straight from the water onto the table. The best way to ensure a good supply of fresh fish is to find a reliable fish store. However, a few basic guidelines will help you. A *really* fresh fish has absolutely no smell. The eyes are bright and clear, the gills are red, and the scales are clean and shiny. The belly of the fish is still hard and elastic; bear in mind that the viscera is the first part to decay.

The following fish are suitable for use in Japanese cooking. Recipes using them appear in the book:

Clam *(Hamaguri):* a popular soup ingredient

Cod *(Tara):* served grilled, simmered and in one-pot dishes

Cod roe *(Tarako)*

Crab *(Kani):* very popular in Japan

Herring *(Nishin):* served grilled, simmered and in one-pot dishes

Mackerel *(Saba):* a round fish; grilled whole or sliced and simmered

Octopus *(Tako):* popular for *sushi,* or vinegared

Oyster *(Kaki):* less of a luxury in Japan, oyster is popular raw, fried or in one-pot dishes

Porgy *(Tai):* a white fleshed flat fish served as *sushi,* grilled and steamed

Salmon *(Sake):* never eaten raw in Japan, but a popular *sashimi* fish in the West.

Scallop *(Hotategai):* served raw or fried

Sea bass *(Suzuki):* served as *sashimi,* grilled and in soups

Shrimp *(Ebi):* particularly popular in Japan, served in many different ways

Sole *(Karei):* served grilled, deep fried or simmered

Squid *(Ika):* very popular, served as *sushi* or cooked

Trout *(Masu):* served as *sashimi* or grilled

Tuna *(Magoro):* one of the most popular *sashimi* fish

ABOVE *Wakame, a nutritious seaweed with long green fronds and a silky texture, is commonly used in soups and salads. Before use, soak for 5 minutes and pare away the tough spine. As a soup ingredient it needs very little cooking. To use in salads, scald with boiling water and immediately refresh with cold water.*

BELOW *One of the most essential items in the Japanese kitchen, bonito flakes (hanu-katsuo) are made from the dried fillet of bonito, a relative of the mackerel, and are used as a basic flavoring for dashi, and as a garnish. Although the best dashi is made with freshly shaved bonito flakes, most Japanese home cooks use ready flaked bonito, which is available in Japanese food shops.*

BELOW *Dried kelp (kombu) is one of the two basic ingredients for dashi, and is also used as a vegetable in its own right. It is sold in Japanese food stores in long dried strips, which should be lightly wiped, not washed, as the flavor is on the surface. Some chefs score the kombu lightly to release the flavor. Kombu should be simmered rather than boiled to avoid bitterness. Store in an airtight container.*

ABOVE *Crisp nori, with its sweet seaweedy taste, appears on most Japanese tables at breakfast time, for it is the seaweed which is rolled around rice, both at home and in sushi bars. Slivered with scissors it serves as a garnish. Before use, nori needs to be lightly toasted over a hot flame for a few seconds, until it changes color and becomes fragrant. Store in an airtight container.*

FOOD FROM THE LAND

The Japanese have a great respect for vegetables; in fact, the Buddhist rule of vegetarianism has led to the development of a sophisticated vegetarian cuisine. Japanese markets abound in vegetables, invariably crisp and fresh. Vegetables are used for their decorative qualities as much as for their taste, and are expected to be perfect in shape as well as quality. Cucumbers are grown in sheaths to make them absolutely straight; and those vegetables that do not reach the highest standards are thrown away. There is an enormous variety of vegetables in Japan, in particular many different types of leafy vegetable, yams and mushrooms. Many of these are unavailable in the West, although some may be found in Indian and West Indian stores or Chinese supermarkets. Japanese chefs working abroad use locally available vegetables to create new dishes along traditional lines, using, for example, celery for burdock.

Generally speaking, Japanese vegetables are smaller and sweeter, thinner skinned and more delicate than their Western counterparts. For Japanese dishes, always select small, young vegetables of the season, immaculately fresh.

Eggplant
Eggplants are much used, in a variety of different types of dishes. They come in many shapes and sizes, all of which are smaller than those available in the West. Small eggplants can sometimes be found in Indian stores.

Bamboo shoots
The shoots of the young bamboo, which grow at an amazing rate, are a symbol of spring in Japan. A very common ingredient throughout the East, they are prized for their crunchiness and delicate taste. Canned bamboo shoots, a rather poor substitute, are available in Chinese and Japanese stores. Once opened, store refrigerated in fresh water.

Burdock
Burdock, a long slender root vegetable with a crunchy texture and earthy taste, is much used in Japanese cooking, particularly in simmered and fried dishes. Fresh burdock may sometimes be found in Japanese food stores; canned burdock is more readily available. Fresh burdock should be scrubbed but not peeled, and immediately immersed in cold water to prevent discoloration.

Chestnuts
Chestnuts large and small are a popular fall food in Japan, roasted and eaten as a snack or included in a variety of sweet and savory dishes. Japanese cooks prefer to peel chestnuts before cooking.

Napa or celery cabbage (*Hakusai*)
Napa cabbage has a somewhat milder flavor than Western cabbage and is much used in Japanese cooking, particularly in one-pot dishes; it also makes a popular pickle. Nowadays it is widely available.

RIGHT *Napa cabbage, widely used in one-pot dishes; daikon radish, which is said to have no calories and is good for the digestion; and scallions, which are an acceptable substitute for Japanese leeks.*

RIGHT *(clockwise) Dried Chinese mushrooms (shiitake); canned bamboo shoots (takenoko); a jar of mixed sushi vegetables; and canned lotus roots.*

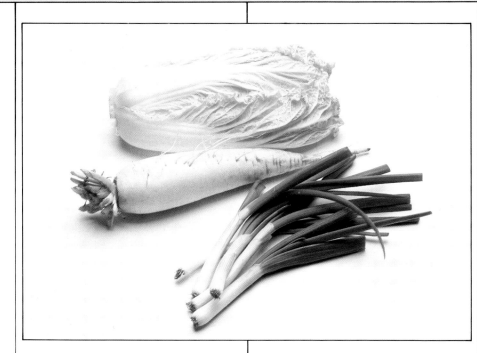

Leeks
The Japanese leek is smaller, sweeter and finer than the Western leek. It is widely used as an ingredient in soups, simmered dishes and grilled dishes and, finely sliced, is a common garnish and condiment. Use long, slender leeks or large scallions.

Lotus root
This crunchy root vegetable is served as *tempura* and in vinegared and simmered dishes. The cross section makes an attractive flower-like garnish. Lotus root is sometimes available fresh in Chinese stores; choose a firm white root and store in a cool, dark place. The root requires long simmering. Canned lotus roots are an acceptable substitute.

Mushrooms
Many different varieties of fresh mushrooms, both wild and cultivated, are used in Japan — in soups, simmered dishes and one-pot dishes. The most common, the *shiitake* mushroom, is used both fresh and dried, and the dried version may be found in Oriental food stores and health food stores. Soak for at least 30 minutes before use and trim away the hard stem; the soaking water may be used for stock. Some varieties of mushroom are available canned in Japanese food stores; otherwise ordinary Western mushrooms may be used as a substitute, although the taste and texture are rather different.

Yams
Many different varieties of yam and sweet potato are used in Japanese cooking in simmered and one-pot dishes and in *tempura*. Sweet potatoes are readily available and are a suitable substitute.

Chrysanthemum leaves
This delicious leaf vegetable is much used in one-pot dishes, particularly in *sukiyaki*. It is sometimes available fresh in oriental food stores. Choose bright green leaves and springy stalks; leaves with buds are too old. Spinach is a possible substitute, but the flavor will be different.

Daikon
Huge white *daikon* roots — a kind of giant white radish — are a common sight in Japanese fields and markets, and the *daikon* has a multitude of uses in Japanese cooking. It is said to have no calories and to be exceptionally good for the digestion; grated, it is served raw as a condiment to counteract the oiliness of deep-fried dishes such as *tempura*. It is a frequent ingredient of simmered and one-pot dishes, and requires relatively long cooking. It is becoming more and more available in Western markets, as well as Chinese and Indian stores, and may be found under the name of *mooli, daikon* or white radish. Select fresh, firm, unwrinkled *daikon*.

Gingko nuts
Gingko nuts have a delicate flavor and texture and are a regular ingredient in *chawan mushi* and other steamed dishes. Fresh gingko nuts can occasionally be found; both the shell and the inner skin should be removed before use. Canned gingko nuts are a poor substitute.

32

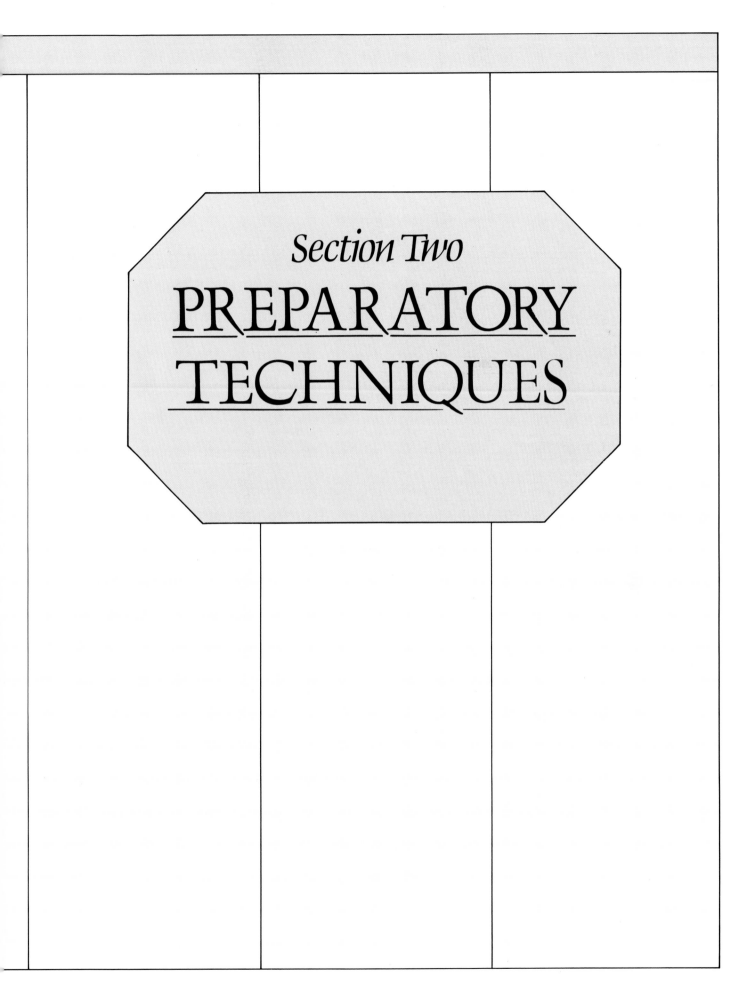

Section Two

PREPARATORY TECHNIQUES

In Japan the great stars of the culinary constellation are the *sashimi* chefs, who jealously guard the secrets of their skills. Although they may be willing to impart their recipes, when it comes to cutting they prefer to give a dazzling display of virtuoso knifework, leaving their apprentices in despair. In Japanese cuisine, with its minimal approach to actual cooking, cutting techniques assume a greater importance than in the West. Foods are transformed more in the cutting than in the cooking. In fact, the preparation of dishes like *sashimi*—served raw—is almost an art form in its own right. The visual appeal for which Japanese cooking is famous depends to a large extent on the quality of the cutting. And the Japanese home cook, while happily experimenting with different cooking methods, will buy ready cut *sashimi* and beef for *sukiyaki,* deeming cutting to be one art best left to the experts.

While we can never hope to emulate the accomplishments of the great chefs who have studied the art of cutting for many years, the basic techniques are quite straightforward and within the reach of any home cook.

PREPARING FISH

Every Japanese supermarket has long counters full of fresh fish, and Japanese cooks gut and fillet fish as a matter of course. In an ordinary home in Japan one may often be served a complete meal from a single fish caught in the ocean that morning, gutted and filleted — the best parts served as *sashimi*, and the head and backbone put to use in the soup.

Small fish look most attractive served whole, and need simply to be gutted. Larger fish are filleted according to their shape.

Preparing fish to be served whole

A fish to be served whole has to be treated carefully so that it keeps its shape. It is important to gut the fish and remove the gills as quickly as possible, to ensure perfect freshness. It is sometimes difficult to gut a fish which is not completely fresh.

Scaling

1 Wash the fish thoroughly in lightly salted water.

2 Holding the head with your left hand, scrape away the scales in short strokes from tail to head, using the back of a knife.

Gutting

1 Open the mouth of the fish, slide in a small sharp knife, and cut the small bone beneath the lower jaw.

2 Insert two chopsticks, one by one, into the fish's mouth to beyond the gills, and twist a few times to catch the stomach and viscera.

3 Carefully pull out the stomach and viscera, trimming to free the gills.

4 Rinse thoroughly with running water.

Preparing fish to be served in fillets

The shape of a fish determines how it should be gutted and filleted. Round-bodied fish such as trout and mackerel are cut along the spine to produce two boneless fillets. Wide flat fish, such as sole, give four thin fillets.

Gutting

1 Wash the fish in lightly salted water and scrape away the scales. Rinse thoroughly and pat dry.

2 Place the fish with the head facing to the left. With a sharp knife, make a diagonal cut at the base of the head. Make a second diagonal cut to remove the head.

3 Slit along the entire belly of the fish and carefully remove the stomach and viscera. Scrape the knife along the inside of the body to break blood pockets. Rinse very thoroughly with cold water.

Two-piece filleting *(Nimai oroshi)*

1 Rest the left hand gently on top of the fish and draw the knife lightly from the head to the tail. Retrace the cut several times, each time cutting closer to the spine; do not use a sawing motion.

2 Turn the fish and cut smoothly from the tail to the head.

3 Cut through to separate the fillets. The fish separates into two halves, one boneless and one containing the backbone.

Three-piece filleting *(Sanmai oroshi)*

1 Follow steps 1–3 of "two-piece filleting".

2 Taking the piece of fish containing the backbone, rest the left hand lightly on the fish and slide the knife between the flesh and the bone from head to tail.

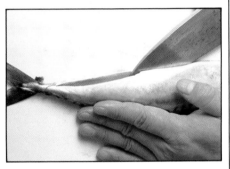

3 Turn the fish and cut through at the base of the tail, drawing the knife along the fish to release the fillet.

4 The fish is in three pieces, two boneless fillets and a backbone with a little flesh.

5 Rinse the fillets and set aside on a flat strainer. If the fillets are not to be used immediately, wrap them in a damp tea towel and refrigerate.

ABOVE *The result of two-piece filleting — one boneless half and one half containing the backbone.*

ABOVE *The result of three-piece filleting — two boneless fillets and a backbone with a little flesh.*

Five-piece filleting *(Gomai oroshi)*
This technique is used for flat fish.

1 | Remove the scales from the top, brown side of the fish. Resting the left hand on the head of the fish, make two deep cuts behind the gills.

2 | Turn the fish and remove the head. Squeeze out the stomach and viscera, and clean out the inside of the body with the tip of the knife. Rinse thoroughly with cold water.

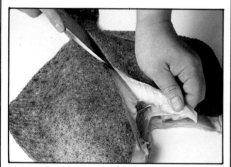

3 | Turn the fish again and cut deeply to the tail, cutting down to the spine.

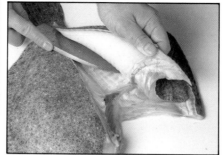

4 | Keeping the edge of the blade flat, slide the knife along the bone—starting from the spinal cut—to release the flesh.

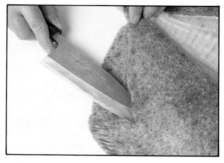

5 | Starting from the tail, slide the knife along the edge of the fish to release the fillet.

6 | Reverse the fish and repeat the procedure to remove the second fillet from the top of the fish.

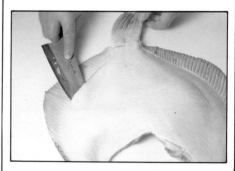

7 | Turn the fish with the white side uppermost and repeat steps 3–6 to remove two more fillets.

8 | The result is four fillets and the lightly fleshed skeleton of the fish. Rinse the fillets and set aside on a flat strainer. Wrap and refrigerate if not for immediate use.

ABOVE *Four fillets and the lightly fleshed skeleton of the fish.*

Salting fish

In Japan fish is almost invariably salted before being cooked, in order to firm the flesh and reduce odor. The quantity of salt and the length of time that the fish is salted vary depending on the fish. Thick fillets need more and longer salting than thin. Fish are usually salted in one of four ways:

Sea water salting *(Tate-jio)*

1 Dissolve 2 Tbsp salt in 5 cups water to make a "sea water" solution.

2 Immerse thin fillets of white fish in the solution for 20 to 30 minutes. Remove and pat dry.

Salt sprinkling *(Furi-jio)*
This is the most popular salting technique, and is used for vegetables and chicken as well as fish.

1 Sprinkle salt evenly over the cutting board. Lay the fish skin-side down on the board. Holding the hand 14in above the fish, sprinkle the fish with salt.

2 Leave the fish for 40–60 minutes; then rinse and pat dry.

Salt dredging *(Beta-jio)*

Dredge the fish in salt and set aside for 60–90 minutes. Rinse and pat dry just before using. This technique is used for very fatty fish, such as mackerel, that need heavy salting.

Paper salting *(Kami-jio)*
This subtle salting technique is used for fish which need minimal salting, usually those which are to be served raw as *sushi* or *sashimi*. Traditionally Japanese handmade paper is used—any absorbent paper such as paper towels will do.

1 Lightly salt a cutting board or plate and cover with a dry sheet of paper. Lay the fish on the paper, cover with a second sheet, and salt again.

2 Leave for 40–60 minutes, so that the fish absorbs a small amount of salt. Carefully remove the fish from the paper and pat dry before using.

PREPARING CHICKEN

Although as Buddhists the Japanese have traditionally refrained from eating four-footed animals, chicken has always been a part of the Japanese diet. As with all foods, chicken which is tender and young is considered to be the best, and is the most suitable for Japanese recipes. The choicest part of the chicken is the tender white meat of the two breast fillets, which are known as bamboo leaf fillets *(sasami)* because of their long leaf-like shape. The breast fillets are usually served raw as *sashimi* with a tasty dipping sauce, or are included in clear soups.

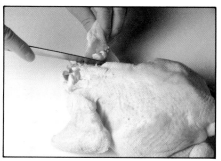

1 To remove the wings, place the chicken with the neck facing towards you. Holding the wing with your left hand, cut deeply around the wing bone to free the wing, then pull the wing firmly and evenly from the carcass. Turn the bird and remove the other wing in the same way.

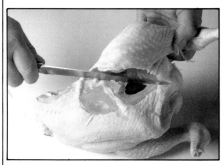

2 To remove the legs, turn the bird on its side and hold one leg in your left hand. Cut deeply between the thigh bone and the carcass and pull the leg away, cutting through the remaining meat. Turn the carcass and remove the other leg in the same way.

continued overleaf

3 To remove the breast meat, turn the carcass upside down and cut deeply along the breast bone to the spine. Turn and repeat on the other side, so that most of the breast meat is released in a single piece from the skeleton.

4 Ease the breast meat from the skeleton and carefully cut through at the tail.

5 To remove the bone from the thigh, cut along the edge of the bone while opening out the flesh. Cut down the other side of the bone and ease it out, leaving the flesh in one piece. Remove the bone from the other leg in the same way. Trim the tough tendons from both legs.

6 The breast fillets *(sasami)* are the two pieces of meat remaining on the carcass, fitting neatly in the hollow of the breast bone and attached to it by white tendons. Cut through the tendons that hold the fillet at one end. Ease the fillet away from the carcass, sliding the knife between the fillet and the carcass. Cut through the remaining tendons to release the fillet. Trim the tough tendons from the fillet.

7 Separate the bony wing from the shoulder, guiding the knife between the bones.

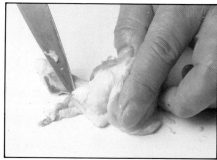

8 Taking the fleshy shoulder meat, slide the knife along each side of the bone to loosen it, leaving it attached to the shoulder at one end.

9 Holding the flesh in your left hand, gently pull the bone so that the flesh is turned to the outside and the skin is on the inside.

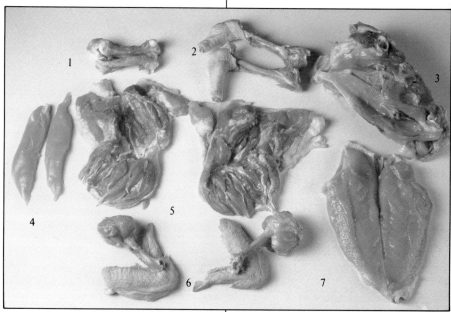

ABOVE *The chicken laid out ready to use: (1) thigh bones; (2) drumstick; (3) carcass; (4) breast fillets; (5) thigh meat; (6) wings and shoulders; (7) breast meat.*

PREPARING DRIED FOODS

The shelves of Japanese foodstores are lined with unfamiliar dried foods: dried mushrooms, seaweeds, and a multi-colored variety of stringy and papery substances. Dried foods are an important part of Japanese cooking and may be easily obtained in the West, making it possible for us to reproduce authentic Japanese tastes. Some of the essential tastes and textures of Japanese cooking are derived from dehydrated vegetables.

In general, dried foods are first rinsed in cold water, then soaked in lukewarm water. After this they are shredded and simmered with fish, meat or vegetables.

Dried shiitake mushrooms

1 Lightly rinse the dried mushrooms and put into lukewarm water to soak.

2 Add a pinch of sugar to bring out the flavor of the mushrooms. They should be soaked for at least 30 minutes. Then trim away the hard stem and drain the mushrooms. The soaking liquid makes a delicious stock which may be used instead of *dashi*. The mushrooms are simmered in seasoned stock or added to a wide variety of different dishes.

Wakame seaweed
One of the most popular seaweeds, *wakame* is used in soups, salads and simmered dishes and as a garnish for *sashimi*.

1 Place the dried *wakame* seaweed in a bowl.

2 Add plenty of lukewarm water and leave to soak for 10 to 15 minutes. The *wakame* will swell up and become a rich glossy green.

3 If the *wakame* is to be used in simmered dishes or as a salad ingredient, it should be drained after soaking and plunged briefly into boiling water to give it a more intense color. Drain again, pat dry and use.

Other seaweeds such as *kombu* and *hijiki* should be soaked in the same way.

Dried gourd strips *(kampyo)*
The large edible gourd provides us with these long, dried, ribbon-like strips which are used as a sort of vegetable string for tying and fastening foods, as well as being simmered with vegetables or fish.

1 Separate out ⅓oz gourd strips and place in a glass or plastic bowl. Sprinkle with 1 tsp salt.

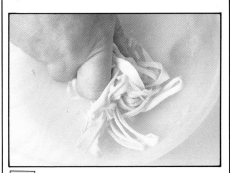

2 Knead the strips thoroughly to soften the fibers.

3 Rinse well and soak in lukewarm water to cover for 15 minutes.

4 Boil in the soaking water until soft. Seasonings should be added after the gourd is cooked.

THE ART OF VEGETABLE CUTTING

It is in the cutting of vegetables that the Japanese cook best displays his virtuousity, transforming in the twinkling of an eye, an eggplant into a fan, a cucumber into a delicate pine leaf and a carrot into a dainty knot. But the various methods of cutting vegetables are not simply decorative. The shaping of each vegetable is appropriate to the vegetable and to the way in which it will be cooked. Thick chunks of vegetable are best for long simmering, while paper-thin slices requiring hardly any cooking go into clear soups. But of course decoratively cut vegetables, shaped to reflect perhaps a particular season or festival, add a great deal to the visual appeal of a dish. And, despite the mystique, most of vegetable cutting techniques are not at all difficult.

The main requirement for vegetable cutting is a good knife. A Japanese vegetable knife is ideal, but any good sharp paring knife will do.

Basic vegetable cutting methods

Circular cuts

1 ROUNDS Cylindrical vegetables like *daikon* radish and carrot are simply sliced through to make rounds.

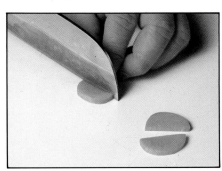

2 HALF-MOON CUT *(Hangetsu giri)* Cut rounds in half to make half moon slices; or halve the vegetable lengthwise and slice.

3 GINGKO LEAVES *(icho giri)* Cut rounds into quarters to make *gingko* leaves. This cut is used for large or tapering vegetables such as bamboo shoots and carrots.

Thick & thin rectangles

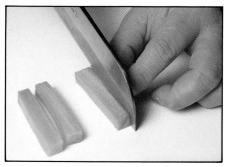

1 CLAPPER CUT *(hyoshigi giri)* Thick rectangles are reminiscent of the wooden blocks clapped together at moments of excitement in Kabuki plays. Cut the vegetable into 2in lengths. Then cut into slices ⅛–⅜in thick. Turn and cut again to make small.

2 POEM CARD CUT *(tanzaku giri)* These thin rectangles are the same shape as the little poem cards which feature in the New Year's festivities. Halve the vegetable and slice into thin slices. Trim into slender rectangles.

Dicing & mincing

1 DICE CUT *(sainome giri)* Cut thick rectangles. Then cut across to make cubes of even size. These dice are about ³⁄₈in.

2 MINCING *(mijin giri)* Shred the vegetable very finely. If the vegetable is thick, first cut into thin strips and then chop very finely, balancing the knife on the point and moving it up and down as you slide the vegetable underneath.

Diagonal, bevel-edged & hexagonal cuts

1 DIAGONAL CUT *(sogi giri)* Long thin vegetables such as leeks, carrots and cucumbers are cut into long or short diagonal slices.

2 BEVEL-EDGED CYLINDERS For long simmering, root vegetables such as sweet potato, *daikon* radish and turnip are sliced across into thick cylinders; the edge is bevelled to make a neat shape.

3 HEXAGONAL CUT *(roppo muki)* Small vegetables such as baby turnips are cut into hexagons for simmering. Cut a slice from the top and base of the vegetable to make it flat, then pare the sides to form a hexagon.

4 SHEET PARING *(katsura muki)* In this technique the vegetable—usually a carrot or *daikon* radish—is peeled in a long continuous motion until it becomes a single large paper-thin sheet. Hold the carrot in your left hand and pare with your right, using the thumb of your right hand to control the knife.

Needle cut, shredding and rinsing

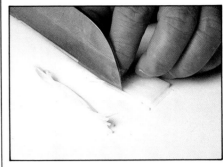

1 NEEDLE CUT *(sen giri)* Cut the vegetable into segments and slice the segments very finely. Cut the slices into very thin threads.

2 PAPER-THIN LEEK SLICES To use as a garnish, the white part of young leeks or scallions are cut into paper-thin slices. The green part of scallions or young leeks are slivered very finely.

The shredded vegetable is then rinsed in cold water, drained and patted dry.

Fancy cutting methods

Slightly more complex cutting methods transform vegetables into delicate garnishes.

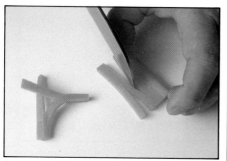

Decorative carrot twist *(matsuka nani)*
Lemon peel as well as carrot is often formed into a decorative twist. Make two thin slits in a slice of carrot and twist.

Pine needles *(Matsuba)*
This particularly beautiful garnish makes use of the contrast of light and dark green in the cucumber.

1 Divide the vegetable into 3in lengths and halve it lengthways. Score the top part of the cucumber very closely with ¼-in deep cuts.

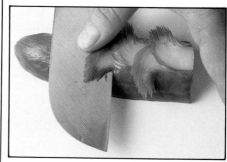

2 Peel back a ¾in strip of skin and push to the side with your thumb. Repeat the cut, pushing the skin to alternate sides to form the pine needles.

ABOVE *Assorted garnishes are relatively easy to make and form an attractive accompaniment to a wide variety of dishes.*

Mountain peaks (yamagata)

Cucumbers or carrots can be turned into little "mountain peaks" to make a decorative garnish.

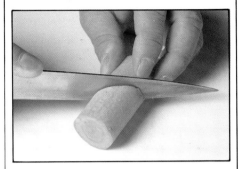

1 Peel the carrot and cut into 3in lengths. Cut lengthways halfway through the vegetable.

2 Make a diagonal cut through to the central cut. Repeat on the other side.

3 Separate the two pieces to make two mountain peaks.

Fan cut (ogi giri)

Cucumbers and eggplants are cut into decorative fans.

1 Trim the base of the eggplant and halve it. Cut each half into quarters.

2 Take one quarter and make lengthways evenly-spaced cuts very close together, leaving ⅓in at one end.

3 Using the blade of a knife and your fingers, press down at the base of the "fan" to spread it open.

Flower cut (hana giri)

Carrots shaped as plum blossoms are a favorite garnish in spring dishes.

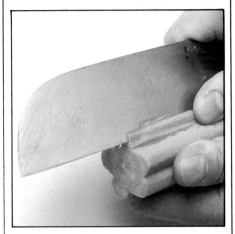

1 Cut the carrot into sections about 3in long and make five lengthways slits. Trim each slit to make the petal shape smooth and round.

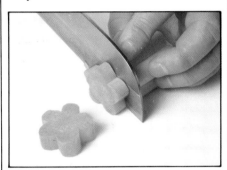

2 Cut slices of the desired thickness. Thick slices are used for simmering and thin slices for garnishes. The slices may be used as they are, or may be pared to make a more sculpted shape.

PLANNING AND PRESENTING THE MEAL

In this book we introduce the basic flavor of Japanese cooking, and hope to convey a little of its spirit. We begin with *dashi*, the essential stock which is considered to be the secret of the Japanese flavor, and then introduce the basic techniques through recipes arranged according to the traditional Japanese order of service. These will be followed by more complex and demanding recipes using these same techniques.

The emphasis throughout is on quality of ingredients and simplicity of cooking techniques. A Japanese meal is designed to provide satisfaction to both the eye and the palete, and the planning and presentation of even the simplest everyday meal is given as much care as the actual preparation.

Planning the menu: selecting and combining dishes

The basis of almost any Japanese meal is rice, some crunchy pickled vegetables and a bowl of thick *miso* soup. To the Japanese way of thinking, this frugal repast provides essential nourishment. All other dishes are considered to be side dishes, to amuse the palate and the eye, and to whet the appetite in anticipation of the serious food, the rice. On this basis the meal can be built up to various degrees of complexity, from the simplest home meal to the most involved restaurant meal.

In contrast to an occidental meal, a Japanese meal has no center, no main course, to be preceded by an hors d'oeuvre and followed by a dessert. At any Japanese meal many small dishes of different types of food will be served, each type of food on its own plate. Many of the dishes will be at room temperature, and will have been prepared several hours beforehand. A sweet dish may be included in the meal, and will be served with, not after, the other dishes.

For a family meal the many dishes are served all at once or in a completely

LEFT *The various dishes making up an individual meal are often served on a lacquered tray or tiny individual table, arranged according to a traditional formula with the rice on the left and the soup on the right, and the other dishes behind them. The chopsticks are laid at the very front, with the tips pointing to the left. At home all the dishes are crowded together on one table, but the traditional placing of dishes is still observed.*

arbitrary order. The table will be crowded with an appetizing array of simmered and grilled fish or vegetables, all carefully arranged in bowls and plates selected to harmonize with the color and shape of the food within, set off with some seasonable garnish. Traditionally an odd number of dishes is served, usually three or five. The arrangement of the menu is structured around cooking methods. The basic traditional menu consists of a soup and three dishes, each cooked by a different method — usually a grilled dish, a simmered dish and perhaps a salad or a steamed dish.

A formal meal, such as one might be served in a restaurant or at a banquet, is a complex variation on the same basic principles. The dishes are served one by one in a particular order determined by cooking method. After some tiny appetizers, a delicate clear soup and some skillfully sliced *sashimi*, the finest and freshest uncooked fish, is served. It is on these that the chef lavishes his attention, and fine *sashimi* is a sure sign of a good meal to follow. After these come a succession of small dishes, with grilled and simmered foods preceding deep-fried dishes and salads. These small dishes may be replaced by a larger item such as a one-pot dish, perhaps *sukiyaki* or *shabu shabu*, accompanied by a couple of side dishes.

Apart from the occasional meal of noodles, all Japanese meals, both family and formal, end with rice, finely sliced pickles and *miso* soup. Dessert, if served at all, will consist of fresh fruit, artistically trimmed.

Variety and balance are the keys to the planning of a Japanese meal. The traditional structure of the meal ensures variety of cooking technique. The simplest menu consists of a soup, a simmered dish, a grilled dish, and a dish representing one other technique, perhaps a steamed dish or a salad, followed by rice and pickles. Dishes based on different techniques can be added to make a more complex meal.

Within this structure, the Japanese cook will ensure balance and variety of ingredients, flavors and textures. Rather than several meat dishes, a meal will consist of a meat dish balanced by fish and perhaps a vegetable. The meal will include both soft and crisp foods. And, in theory at least, the classic Five Tastes of oriental tradition — hot, sweet, sour,

salty and bitter — will be represented.

The truly distinguishing feature of Japanese cooking is not the culinary so much as what we might call the aesthetic or even the spiritual aspect. As Japanese life is intimately linked to the passing of the seasons, so too is the daily food. Warming one-pot dishes, communally cooked, are appropriate to winter, while chilled dishes and salads are served in the summer. Seasonal ingredients are used, not simply because they are the freshest, but to evoke a pleasing awareness of the season.

The Japanese cook selects ingredients according to the time of year, taking into account also the visual possibilities of each, to ensure variety of shape and color in the meal. The various ingredients serve as a palate with which the cook will create his transient work of art.

Following are some typical family menus composed from recipes in this book:

Breakfast
Steamed or simmered vegetables
Tsukemono (pickled vegetables)
Plain boiled rice
Miso soup
Green tea

Lunch
Chirashi zushi (assorted *sushi* on rice)
Nasu no itame-ni (simmered eggplant)
Tsukemono (pickled vegetables)
Fresh fruit

Dinner
Beef *teriyaki* (grilled beef)
Saba nitsuke (simmered mackerel)
Yuzen ae (chicken and kiwi fruit salad)
Chawan mushi (steamed savory
   custard)
Plain boiled rice
Fresh fruit
Green tea

Supper
Sashimi (sliced uncooked fish)
Tempura (deep fried prawns or shrimps
   and vegetables in batter)
Shirazu ae (mixed vegetable salad with
   tofu dressing)
Plain boiled rice
Clear soup
Green tea

The presentation of the meal

Japanese food is famous as much for its appearance as for its taste, perhaps more so. In Japan a great chef is also a great artist, with food as his palate. Ever since the days of Prince Genji, subject of the world's first novel written a thousand years ago, aesthetics has played a central role in Japanese society. Not only the chefs of the great restaurants, but every cook preparing a meal for the family at home gives as much care and thought to the visual quality of the finished meal as to its preparation.

In Japan the creation of a meal as a work of art is surrounded by mystique. Chefs like to dazzle their apprentices with the speed of their cutting, wielding their knife like a samurai sword to produce the most delicate flowers from unpromising materials like hard-cooked eggs or carrots, or slicing beef into impossibly thin slices to be spread out with a flourish like flower petals. We Westerners cannot hope to master such an art without years of practice. But we can at least become more aware of the visual possibilities of food.

Just as every tiny Japanese poem — *haiku* — contains a reference to the season, so too in the planning and presentation of a Japanese meal awareness of the season is all important. The various seasonal ingredients must be perfectly formed: misshapen strawberries will be thrown away, no matter how sweet they might be. Foods are usually cooked as lightly as possible to conserve their color and shape; green vegetables are refreshed in cold water to enhance the color.

Tableware appropriate to the season, the meal and the particular food is selected with great care, the key note being harmony. *Sashimi* is served on particularly beautiful dishes, formed into a miniature landscape for the spring festival. Every Japanese home contains a great variety of tableware, in sets of five rather than our half dozen. Within one place setting, the cardinal rule is that no dish should match any other. Rice and soup are served in red or black lacquered wooden bowls with lids. Plates for the side dishes may be round, square, oblong, assymetrical, or even shaped like a Japanese fan. In fall a perfect red and

ABOVE *The setting of the meal is a Japanese room, with its muted colors and sparse furnishings, creating an atmosphere of harmony and stillness.*

gold leaf may be used as a plate to give a seasonal touch. There are tiny dishes for pickles and garnishes, handleless lidded cups for *chawan mushi* (a custardy soup), and big bowls for *donburi,* rice with a meat and vegetable topping. Noodles are served in big bowls in winter and chilled in a bamboo basket in summer. *Tempura* too may be served in a delicate bamboo basket. Dishes are of varying sizes, shapes, materials and textures, and some may be treasured heirlooms.

Each member of the family has his own chopsticks, made of bamboo or lacquered wood and kept in a box with a sliding lid like a pencil case. Guests are always given disposable chopsticks, made of one piece of bamboo and still joined together to show that they have never been used before. Chopsticks are laid neatly at each plate with the tip resting on a small decorative chopstick rest.

A whole class of food is served ready prepared in lacquered wooden boxes with a section for each item. And a set of special stacking boxes together with an ornate lacquered *sake* flask and matching cups is reserved for the ceremonial New Year's meal.

Within the dish the food itself is very

TOP *Food is always carefully arranged within a dish. For example, grilled fish should always face to the left with the tail slightly away from the diner.* ABOVE <u>*Sashimi*</u> *is often presented on a tray, beautifully arranged and surrounded with garnishes.*

carefully arranged, always in much smaller quantities than we serve in the West. The main points to bear in mind are; 1) pleasing arrangement, and 2) asymmetry. Foods do not usually fill the whole dish, but are artistically placed in the center. Grilled fish face to the left, the tail slightly away from the diner. Simmered foods are served with the largest item at the back of the dish. Foods to be cooked at the table, like one-pot dishes and *tempura,* are prepared beforehand and arranged on huge platters, with foods of each type placed together.

Most Japanese dishes are attractively garnished to give a contrast of both taste and color. Some of the most common garnishes are grated white radish *(daikon),* grated fresh ginger, slivered leeks, sesame and poppy seeds, and tiny *kinome* leaves (prickly ash). The cutting and coloring of vegetables and gluten to form flowers or maple leaves is an art in its own right, and such garnishes give a seasonable touch to many dishes.

HOW TO MAKE TEA
(O-cha)

Tea is an essential part of both the Japanese way of life and the Japanese meal. Certain rules of etiquette govern the making, serving and drinking of even the simplest cup of tea, and powdered tea is the basis of the extraordinarily complex and fascinating tea ceremony.

Tea is drunk throughout the day, and when guests call they are always welcomed with a cup of tea and a cake. When the diner enters a restaurant tea is immediately served, and often continues to be served throughout the meal.

Japanese tea is green tea, made with the green unfermented leaves of the tea plant. Between Osaka and Tokyo, in the Shizuoka region, the hills are covered with row upon row of tea bushes (indeed the finest tea is said to come from Uji, near Kyoto). There are many grades of tea. *Bancha,* the coarsest grade of tea, contains stems as well as leaves, and big mugs of *bancha* are served free of charge throughout the meal in most restaurants. Standard everyday tea is somewhat finer. *Sencha* is a particularly fine grade of leaf tea, reserved for special occasions and special guests and served in small porcelain cups. *Shincha,* "new tea", is made from the young leaves of the tea plant in spring. *Macha* is the tea used for the tea ceremony; it is a brilliant green powder which is whisked to a foam with a small bamboo whisk and served according to the rules of a complex etiquette.

Japanese tea is made not with boiling water but with water just a little hotter than drinking temperature. If the tea is left to steep it quickly becomes bitter. Both teapots and teacups are tiny and are usually made of porcelain. It is customary to fill the cup only two-thirds full so that the rim of the cup may be held without burning the drinker's fingers.

1 Warm the teapot and put 1 heaping teaspoon of leaves per person into the pot.

2 Pour boiled water which has been allowed to cool a little over the tea-leaves. Cover the pot and allow to steep for 1–2 minutes. Warm the teacups and, holding down the lid of the teapot, fill the teacups two-thirds full.

3 To drink the tea, pick up the cup with your right hand and support it on your left. It is customary to make a slight slurping noise when drinking tea, particularly if it is hot.

SAKE

As old as Japan itself, *sake* is the national alcoholic drink and is clearly the most appropriate to accompany a Japanese meal. The exchange of cups of *sake* signifies the sealing of the marriage in the wedding ceremony. Furthermore, *sake* is the most acceptable offering to the Shinto deities, and in front of any Shinto shrine you will see endless kegs of *sake* neatly stacked in rows.

Sake is made by fermenting freshly steamed white rice. Once the fermentation period is completed, the *sake* can be drunk immediately—it does not need to mature. As with wine, different parts of Japan produce different types of *sake*, and *sake* is actually graded according to quality. For our purposes the most important distinction to be made is between sweet and dry *sake*. Sweet *sake* is considered to be superior and more natural than the dry variety. *Sake* is also used for cooking as well as for drinking, and is usually sold in huge bottles. It should be stored in a cool dark place and, once opened, should be drunk quite quickly.

In the summer *sake* may be drunk cold and it is often served in small square wooden boxes instead of cups. However, *sake* is more often served warm, since the warming process excentuates its delicate flavor. To heat *sake*, pour some from the bottle into a small flask and put the flask in a saucepan over a low flame. Heat the *sake* slowly until it is a little hotter than blood heat—never boil *sake*. Carefully dry the flask before setting it on the table.

ABOVE RIGHT *Sake is served in small flasks and drunk in very small ceramic cups. Always raise your cup to receive sake, supporting the cup on your left hand and holding it with your right.* RIGHT *The etiquette of sake-drinking requires that you fill your neighbor's cup but never your own. In Japan a sake cup is never allowed to remain empty for long. The cup may be filled to the very brim. Sake should, in theory, be downed in one. The toast is 'Campai!'.*

ABOVE *Sake* contributes largely to the convivial atmosphere of meals such as *teppan yaki* (mixed grill) which are cooked before the diners. Throughout the meal flasks of warmed *sake* are always on hand and are constantly replenished.

DINING THE JAPANESE WAY

The Japanese meal is designed not simply to fill the stomach but also to satisfy the eye and the spirit. In a Japanese room, the atmosphere is one of harmony and stillness. Floors are covered in thick straw matting, *tatami,* which is slightly resilient underfoot. Paper-covered windows diffuse the light to give a soft glow, and sliding doors of thick textured paper close off the room. The meal is laid out on low tables about the height of a coffee table. At home one table is used for the whole family, while in a restaurant a small table is provided for each diner. Diners kneel or sit on thin flat cushions on the floor. At each place is a bamboo basket containing a small damp towel, tightly rolled, steaming hot in winter and icy cold in summer. The diners wipe their hands and faces, and even the back of their necks. If the meal is a formal one, the host or hostess may serve a cup of tea or a small cake. The dishes which are served at room temperature are already arranged on the table. Before beginning to eat the diners murmur *"Itadakimasu",* meaning "I receive", a brief expression of gratitude to both the deities and the host or hostess for providing food.

In Japan, as in every country in the world, there is an accepted code of behavior at the table, and while it is not necessary to follow all the rules of Japanese etiquette, some knowledge may enhance one's enjoyment of a Japanese meal. The essence of Japanese etiquette is simply to appreciate the care which has gone into the creation of the meal and to eat it with awareness and respect as well as enjoyment.

Using Chopsticks

1 At each place is a pair of chopsticks, the pointed tips facing to the left and resting on a small decorative chopstick rest. Chopsticks to be used at table are often made of bamboo or lacquered wood, with an ornate design.

2 Take the chopsticks in your right hand as follows: hold one chopstick with your thumb and first two fingers as if holding a pencil—this is the chopstick which will be moved. Slide the second chopstick behind your thumb to rest between your second and third fingers—this chopstick remains still. With a little practice you will quickly acquire the knack of manipulating chopsticks.

Eating With Chopsticks

1 When eating the main part of the meal preceding the rice, leave your bowl or plate on the table and pick up each item of food with chopsticks. When taking food from a communal dish, either use separate serving chopsticks or reverse your own chopsticks. Put the food from the communal dish into your own bowl, and then eat directly from your bowl.

2 When eating rice, pick up the rice bowl and rest it on your left hand, taking the rice using the chopsticks in your hand.

Soup

1 Soup is usually served in a lacquered bowl with a high domed lid. As the hot soup cools it creates a suction force which holds the lid to the bowl. To release the lid, gently squeeze the bowl and lift the lid.

2 Pick up the soup bowl and rest it on your left hand. Use chopsticks to pick out and eat the solid ingredients.

3 Resting the bowl on your left hand and holding it with your right, raise the bowl to your lips like a cup and drink the soup directly from the bowl. It is customary to make a slurping sound as you drink soup, particularly if it is hot.

Common Mistakes

Just as the meal has been created with care, so it should be eaten with care. The following mistakes are not serious, but they may detract from the elegance of the presentation.

1 Never leave the chopsticks in the rice.

2 Always return the chopsticks to their rest between mouthfuls, and do not lay them on the bowls or plates.

3 Always hold the soup bowl with two hands, not one.

4 Always hold items of food *between* the two chopsticks; never pierce a piece of food with the chopsticks.

A JAPANESE MEAL

In Japan, a tiny three or five line poem—*haiku, senryu* or *tanka*—encapsulates a whole experience in the fewest possible words. A poet of the last century, on being confronted with a Western meal, wrote a *senryu* which roughly translated reads, "Western food—every single plate is round!". Having taken your place at table you will find before you something rather different from a traditional Western meal on its single, large plate. Every Japanese meal, no matter how simple, is prepared with the utmost care, the primary aim being to provide delight both to the tongue and eye. While Japanese cuisine is undoubtably one of the healthiest in the world, this is almost accidental since nutritional considerations have not traditionally played much part in the planning of a meal. Each item of food is chosen for its perfection of form as well as its freshness, and is arranged in an aesthetically pleasing fashion on the plate. While every place setting is identical, within each place setting every item of china is different. The plates and bowls are selected to provide variety of shape, color, material and even texture, and to complement the visual qualities of the food which they contain.

When the diners have taken their places and refreshed themselves by wiping their hands and faces with the small steaming towel which is folded at each place, they are served first the hor d'oeuvre (*zensai*). This consists of tiny portions of a variety of seasonal delicacies—fresh shrimps, morsels of squid and minute portions of an assortment of vegetables—all exquisitely shaped and elegantly arranged on the plate. The preparation of hors d'oeuvres is largely left to professional chefs in Japan; the home cook will normally omit the hors d'oeuvre or simply serve a light vinegared salad instead.

The hors d'oeuvre is followed by two apparently simple dishes which, to the Japanese gourmet, constitute the high point of the meal. A delicate clear soup (*suimono*), in which tiny morsels of seafood and vegetables hang suspended, is served in the finest of lacquer bowls, usually red or black, and topped with a domed lid. This is accommpanied by *sashimi*, gleamingly fresh raw fish of

several different varieties, which is truly the highlight of the meal. The fish is cut into succulent slices, and one portion typically consists of two or three slices of each variety of fish, beautifully garnished with perhaps a seasonal leaf or a few slices of cucumber decoratively cut. It is on the clear soup and the *sashimi* that the chef's reputation rests, and the tiny portions are savored and the dishes removed before the following course is served.

The central part of the meal consists of a variety of small dishes representing each of the different techniques of Japanese cooking. Even in the simplest of family meals there is usually a grilled dish and a simmered dish. The diners may be served with a slice of grilled fish or a small whole fish, cunningly arranged on the plate to resemble a fish leaping through the waves. A dish of vegetables, lightly simmered and still crisp and colorful, will be served in a deep bowl. The grilled and simmered dishes are frequently served at room temperature. During the meal some hot dishes, perhaps a savory steamed custard (*chawan mushi*) in a small cup with a lid and some crisp deep-fried fish or seafood, may be served. Very soft foods, such as *chawan mushi*, are eaten with a spoon and the lid of the cup is replaced to indicate that the dish is finished.

In the winter, be it in a restaurant or a private home, the central part of the meal may consist of a one-pot dish

ABOVE *The classic* shabu shabu, *one of Japan's most famous dishes.* RIGHT *A formal Japanese banquet.*

(*nabemono*). Some of Japan's most famous dishes, such as *sukiyaki* and *shabu shabu*, are one-pot dishes. The table is loaded with platters of immaculately fresh vegetables or paper thin slices of the finest beef, and formality is forgotten as the diners help in the cooking, taking cooked foods directly from the cooking pot. Some restaurants are designed solely for one-pot cooking, with tables consisting of great iron griddles heated from beneath. *Sake* is an essential accompaniment of such meals, and the evening is likely to end with singing.

When all the dishes are cleared away, rice is served, steaming hot, in small white porcelain bowls. A few hot or salty pickles are eaten with the rice, and a bowl of *miso* soup completes the meal. It is considered quite unforgivable to leave even a single grain of rice, for rice is food itself and should never be wasted. The meal is followed by green tea and tiny portions of fresh fruit, artistically cut into bite size pieces and served with a tiny fork or toothpick. Fruit is never picked up with the fingers.

When the meal finally ends, the diners murmur *"Gochiso sama deshita"*, to express their appreciation of the meal to both the deities and the host or hostess or even the waitress. Even after receiving a simple cup of tea it is customary to give thanks in this way.

A FORMAL BANQUET

1. Hors d'oeuvre

2. Clear soup

3. Raw fish

4. Grilled dish

A one-pot dish may stand in for 4, 5, 6 & 7

6. Simmered dish

5. Steamed dish

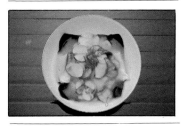

7. Deep-fried dish

8. Vinegared salad

9.Rice 10.Miso soup 11.Pickles

12. Green tea

13. Fresh fruit

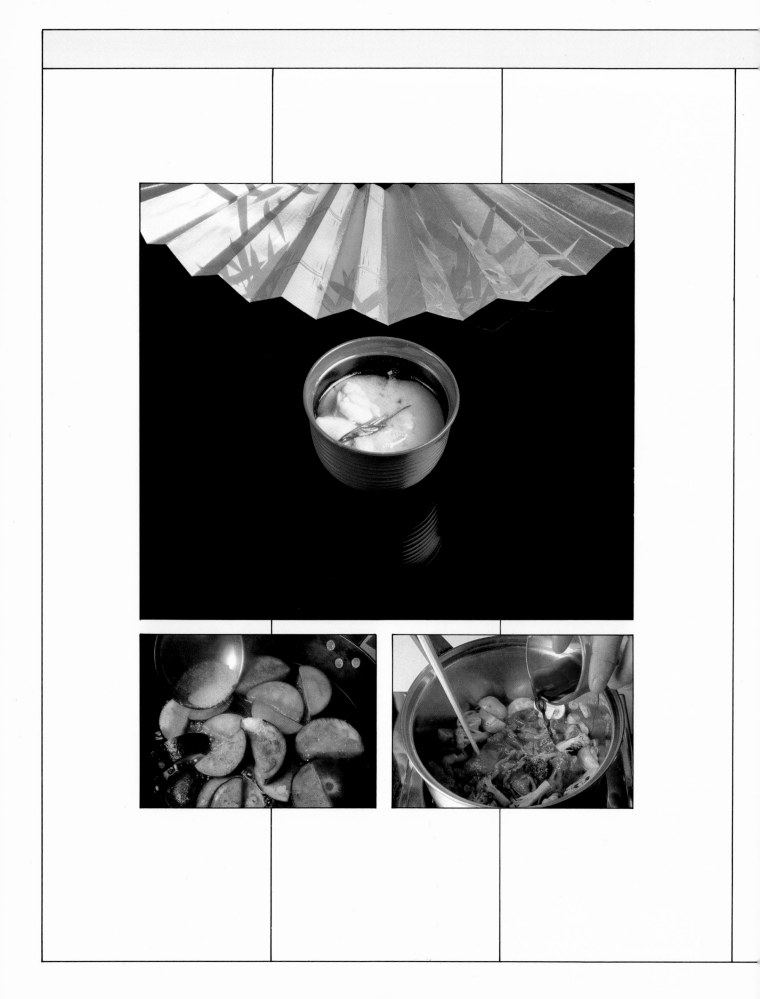

Section Three

STEP-BY-STEP RECIPES

BASIC STOCK
Dashi

The characteristic flavor which distinguishes Japanese food depends largely on *dashi*, accented perhaps with soy sauce or *sake*. *Dashi* is the basic stock which is used in some way in nearly every Japanese dish, and before preparing a meal making it is always the cook's first task. The flavorings for *dashi* are *kombu* seaweed and dried bonito flakes. *Dashi* can vary in quality from that made with the best Hokkaido *kombu* and freshly shaved bonito flakes, to the instant supermarket version, and the flavor of the dishes made with each *dashi* vary accordingly.

DASHI I

Dashi I is a light stock subtly flavored with fresh *kombu* and bonito, used for clear soups.

INGREDIENTS (Serves 4-6)
4½ cups cold water
4 in piece <u>kombu</u> seaweed
1 Tbsp dried bonito flakes

1 Put 4½ cups cold water in a large saucepan and add the *kombu*. Bring slowly to a boil. Remove the *kombu* just before the water boils, and reserve to use in *Dashi II*.

2 Add the *bonito* flakes. Bring the water to a full boil and immediately remove from the heat. Allow the flakes to settle.

3 Strain off the bonito flakes through a cheesecloth-lined sieve. Reserve the bonito flakes to use in *Dashi II*.

DASHI II

Dashi II is a heavier stock, made by simmering the *kombu* and bonito that have been used to make *Dashi I*. It is used for simmered dishes, seasoned stocks and *miso* soups, where a stronger flavor is required.

INGREDIENTS (Serves 6)
7½ cups cold water
<u>kombu</u> and bonito flakes reserved from
  Dashi I
1 Tbsp dried bonito flakes

1 Put the reserved *kombu* and bonito flakes with the cold water in a large saucepan and heat just to a boil. Lower the heat and simmer for about 20 minutes, until the stock is reduced by a third.

2 Add the dried bonito flakes and immediately remove the saucepan from the heat. Allow the flakes to settle, then strain off through a cheesecloth-lined sieve.

THICK SOUPS
Shirumono

Almost every Japanese meal includes a soup — ranging from staples like the *miso* soup, with which many Japanese start the day, and the thick broths which are almost a meal in themselves, to the elegant clear soups served as part of a restaurant meal. These epitomize the simple preparation and sophisticated aesthetic which characterize Japanese cooking.

There are two main types of soup in Japanese cooking: clear soups and thick soups. Soup is always served piping hot, in a red or black lacquered bowl. A domed lid helps to retain heat.

The grand finale of any Japanese meal is rice, a few pickles and a bowl of *miso* soup. These three constitute the basis of the meal, providing ample nourishment in themselves. Indeed, to the Japanese mind, a perfectly adequate meal consists only of these. To this day, most Japanese begin the day with a warming and nourishing bowl of *miso* soup, and there are as many varieties of this soup as there are days in the year. Whole cookbooks in Japan are devoted solely to *miso* soup.

Basically, white *miso* is lighter and sweeter and tends to be used more in summer soups. Red *miso* is thicker and saltier, more suitable for thick winter broths. Miso is always creamed in a little hot stock and added to the soup just before serving. Once the *miso* is added the soup should not be boiled, as this changes the taste of the *miso* and destroys the living enzymes.

MISO SOUP WITH WAKAME AND TOFU
(Wakame to tofu no miso shiru)

In this classic *miso* soup, the *tofu* is very lightly simmered in the *dashi*, to give a slightly firmer consistency.

INGREDIENTS (Serves 4)
8 in piece dried wakame seaweed
8oz tofu
3 ¾ cups Dashi II
3 Tbsp red miso

1 Rinse the *wakame* and soak in lukewarm water for 10 to 15 minutes. Drain and cut into 1in pieces. Cut the *tofu* into cubes.

2 Bring the *dashi* to a boil, add the *wakame* and *tofu* and simmer for just 1 minute. Ladle a little of the hot *dashi* into a bowl, and cream the *miso*.

3 Strain the *miso* into the hot *dashi;* do not reboil. Ladle the soup into four warmed soup bowls, distributing the *tofu* and *wakame* evenly, and serve immediately.

MISO SOUP WITH MUSHROOMS AND LEEKS
(Shiitake to negi no miso shiru)

There are many different varieties of mushroom in Japan, ranging from small grey clumps of *nameko* mushrooms to big, wild mushrooms rather like cepes. Any kind of mushroom makes a welcome addition to *miso* soup. For this recipe you may use fresh mushrooms, reconstituted dried mushrooms or, best of all, wild mushrooms.

INGREDIENTS (Serves 4)
4 large or 8 small mushrooms
1 young leek
3 ¾ cups Dashi II
3 Tbsp white miso

1 Wipe the mushrooms, trim away the hard stem, and slice the caps finely. Wash the leek, pat dry, and slice very finely.

2 Bring the *dashi* to the boil, add the mushrooms, and simmer for just 30 seconds. Ladle a little of the hot dashi into a bowl and cream the *miso* into it.

3 Strain the *miso* mixture into the hot *dashi;* do not reboil. Ladle the soup into four warmed soup bowls, distributing the mushrooms evenly. Sprinkle over a little chopped leek and serve immediately.

MISI SOUP WITH TOFU AND LEEKS
(*Tofu to negi no miso shiru*)

This *miso* soup is a breakfast favorite and can be prepared in a very short time. *Tofu* and leeks sliced very finely need no precooking.

INGREDIENTS (Serves 4)
1 young leek
8oz tofu
3 ¾ cups Dashi II
3 Tbsp red miso

2 Heat the *dashi* in a small saucepan. Put a little of the hot *dashi* in a bowl, add the *miso* and soften with a wire whisk. Strain the *miso* mixture into the hot *dashi*. Do not reboil.

3 Ladle the *dashi* over the *tofu* and leeks in each bowl and serve immediately.

1 Wash the leek and slice very finely; divide among four soup bowls. Cut the *tofu* into small cubes and distribute among the four bowls.

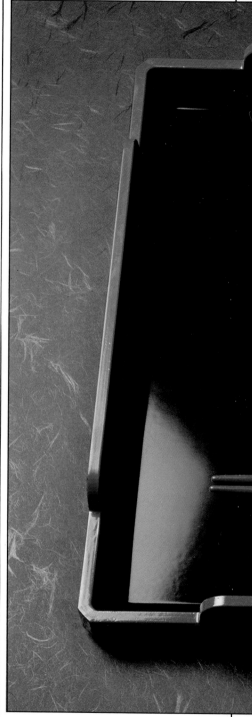

THICK VEGETABLE SOUP WITH TOFU
(*Kaminari jiru*)

This thick nourishing soup, full of traditional Japanese vegetables, is an ideal winter dish. The *tofu* should be well drained so that it can absorb the tasty stock.

INGREDIENTS (Serves 4)
8oz <u>*tofu*</u>
2 medium carrots
3 medium potatoes
1 bamboo shoot, fresh or tinned
8 fresh or dried & reconstituted <u>*shiitake*</u>
   mushrooms
1 cake <u>*konnyaku*</u> *(arum root)*
2 Tbsp vegetable oil
3 ¾ cups <u>*Dashi II*</u>
4 Tbsp red <u>*miso*</u>

1 First drain the *tofu:* set a weight such as a chopping board or dinner plate on the *tofu* and set aside for at least 30 minutes to drain.

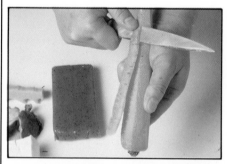

2 Prepare the vegetables. Wash and peel the carrots and potatoes and cut into small chunks. Cut the bamboo shoot into pieces of the same size. Trim away the hard stems of the mushrooms and cut into quarters.

3 With a teaspoon, cut the *konnyaku* into chunks. Heat the vegetable oil in a frying pan, add the vegetables and sauté over high heat, until lightly browned and evenly coated with oil.

4 Turn the vegetables into a saucepan and ladle the *dashi* over them. Bring to a boil. Squeeze the drained *tofu* through your fingers and into the soup. Ladle a little of the hot soup into a bowl and add the *miso.* Soften with a wire whisk.

5 Strain the *miso* into the soup. Reheat the soup until nearly boiling, but do not boil. Ladle the soup into warmed soup bowls and serve immediately.

THICK NEW YEAR'S SOUP WITH CHICKEN AND RICE CAKES *(Ozoni)*

New Year is the great annual festival in Japan, the equivalent of our Christmas. On New Year's morning, after the traditional toast with *sake,* the first meal of the year is a filling bowl of soup with a sticky rice cake *(mochi)* at the bottom of each bowl. Rice cakes are one of the great festive foods of Japan; in the old days the whole family used to participate in the pounding of the sticky rice. Rice cakes are perhaps an acquired taste; it may be best to begin one's acquaintance with only a quarter of a rice cake.

INGREDIENTS (Serves 4)
4 rice cakes
8oz boned chicken, leg and breast,
  with skin
2 young leeks
3 ¾ cups Dashi II
3 Tbsp white miso

1 Broil the rice cakes under a hot broiler or over a hot flame, turning so that the cakes do not burn. When the surface is crisp and brown, remove from the heat and pierce with a fork a few times.

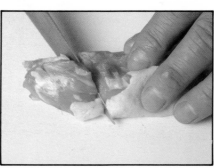

2 Trim the chicken and slice into thin strips. Blanch in a little lightly salted water for 2 minutes, and drain. Slice the leeks diagonally into fine slices.

3 In a large saucepan, bring the *dashi* to a boil; add the chicken pieces and simmer until tender.

4 Ladle a little of the hot soup into a bowl, add the *miso* and soften with a wire whisk. Strain the *miso* into the soup. Reheat the soup but do not boil.

5 Warm four soup bowls and put a rice cake into each. Ladle the soup into the bowls, distributing the chicken pieces evenly. Top with thin slices of leek and serve immediately.

ABOVE *New Year's soup is served in a lidded lacquered bowl colored red, the color of happiness and good luck. Also shown is a decorative bat for playing a special New Year's game similar to badminton.*

CLEAR SOUPS
Suimono

A clear soup is composed almost like a picture — a morsel of seafood, perfect in shape and color; a sprig of greenery to provide contrast; a delicate twist of citrus peel. All hang suspended in a bowl of shimmering clear soup.

Clear soups are traditionally composed, like a flower arrangement, from three basic elements: the main ingredient, "the host", consists of lightly parboiled fish, seafood or chicken, chosen to reflect the season; the complementary ingredient, "the guest", may consist of a green vegetable, a few mushrooms or some seaweed. Finally, ginger juice, a tiny piquant leaf or a shred of lemon peel, provides a fragrant garnish. Clear soups, with their pure taste, must always be made from the best and freshest *dashi*.

EGG DROP SOUP WITH SNOW PEAS
(Tamago to kinusaya no suimono)

This delicate clear soup with its filaments of beaten egg is very popular in Japan.

INGREDIENTS (Serves 4)
4oz snow peas
3 ¾ cups Dashi I
½ tsp light soy sauce
salt
2 eggs

1 Wash the snow peas, pat dry, and slice diagonally into very thin slices. Parboil in lightly salted water for 1 minute, remove and plunge into cold water to stop further cooking. Drain and pat dry.

2 Bring the *dashi* just to a boil; turn the heat to low and season to taste with soy sauce and salt. Beat the eggs lightly in a small bowl.

3 Add the peas to the simmering *dashi,* and pour over the egg in a thin stream. Remove from heat immediately and ladle into warmed soup bowls.

CLEAR SOUP WITH CHICKEN AND LEEKS
(Tori to negi no suimono)

In this soup the chicken is briefly simmered in the *dashi* to give it a subtle flavor.

INGREDIENTS (Serves 4)
4oz boned chicken breast
salt
4 dried <u>shiitake</u> mushrooms
1 tsp sugar
1 young leek
3 ¾ cups <u>Dashi I</u>

1 Trim away the gristle from the chicken and cut into bite size pieces. Salt lightly and simmer in water to cover until the pieces are tender.

2 Wash the mushrooms and soak in lukewarm water with the sugar for 20 minutes. Remove, trim away the tough stem, and slice the caps finely. Wash the leek and slice very finely.

3 Place the chicken and mushrooms in a saucepan, add the *dashi*, bring to a boil, and simmer for 5 minutes, until the mushrooms are tender. Remove the chicken and mushroom slices from the *dashi* with chopsticks.

4 Arrange the chicken and mushrooms in four warmed soup bowls, distributing them evenly. Ladle the hot *dashi* over the chicken and mushrooms in each bowl, sprinkle over a few slices of leek, and serve immediately.

CLEAR SOUP WITH CLAMS
(Hamaguri ushio-jiru)

This clear soup featuring clams in their shells is a dish for festive occasions in Japan. *Dashi* is not used in this soup; instead the water in which the clams are gently simmered becomes a delicately-flavored stock. The clams for this dish should be of the best quality and as fresh as possible; in Japan only live (not canned) clams are used.

INGREDIENTS (Serves 4)
4 large hard-shelled clams
3 ¼ cups cold water
4 x 4in piece <u>kombu</u> seaweed
pinch of salt
small bunch curly parsely
4 pieces <u>yuzu</u> or lemon peel

1 Put the clams in lightly salted water to cover and leave in a dark place for 4-5 hours. Wash the clams thoroughly, wipe the *kombu* and put in a saucepan with the cold water.

2 Bring to a boil, adding 1tsp salt just before the water boils. Remove the *kombu* and discard. Simmer for 2 minutes, until the clams open. Remove the pan from the heat.

3 Remove the clams and separate the clam meat from the shells with a sharp paring knife. Wash the shells and arrange one shell in each soup bowl. Place a clam in each shell.

4 Wash the curly parsley, pat dry and arrange in the four bowls. Lay a slice of *yuzu* or lemon rind in each bowl. Strain the stock and reheat, adding a little salt to taste. Ladle the hot stock carefully into the soup bowls and serve immediately.

CLEAR SOUP WITH SEA BASS
(*Suzuki no suimono*)

A slightly thicker clear soup with root vegetables is suitable for winter.

INGREDIENTS (Serves 4)
4 1 x 1 in slices of sea bass
salt
½ small carrot
1oz <u>daikon</u> radish
3 ¾ cups <u>Dashi I</u>
a few slivers lemon rind

1 Lightly salt the pieces of sea bass, and simmer gently in water to cover until the flesh is tender.

2 Trim and scrape the carrot and *daikon* radish and cut into thick rectangles ("Clapper cut" — *see page 40*). Parboil in lightly salted water until just tender.

3 Arrange the sea bass pieces and vegetables attractively in four warmed bowls. Heat the *dashi* just to boiling point and ladle into the bowls, taking care not to disturb the arrangement. Float a few slivers of lemon rind on top of each bowl and serve immediately.

CLEAR SOUP WITH SHRIMPS AND SPINACH
(*Ebi no suimono*)

In this classic clear soup the shrimps and spinach are precooked and carefully arranged in the bowl and the hot *dashi* is poured over them. The shrimp is shaped into a decorative "flower".

INGREDIENTS (Serves 4)
4 medium raw shrimps
salt
3 Tbsp <u>kuzu</u>, potato flour or cornstarch
¼ cup spinach leaves
3 ¾ cups <u>Dashi I</u>
a few slivers <u>yuzu</u> or lemon rind

1 Shell and devein the shrimps, leaving the tail attached. Wash and pat dry.
  Slit the back of the shrimps open and press out flat.

2 Cut a lengthways slit in the middle and push the tail through this slit to make a shrimp "flower". Repeat with the remaining shrimps.

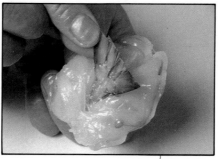

3 Salt the shrimps lightly, and dredge in *kuzu* or cornstarch. Drop the shrimps into lightly salted boiling water and parboil for 2 minutes. Drain on paper towels.

4 Wash the spinach and parboil in lightly salted boiling water for 2 minutes, until just tender. Plunge immediately into cold water to retain the brilliant green color

5 Lay the leaves of spinach evenly on a bamboo rolling mat and roll firmly to squeeze out moisture. Unroll the spinach from the bamboo mat and cut it into four 2in pieces.

6 Warm four soup bowls and arrange a roll of spinach in each. Arrange a shrimp beside each roll of spinach.

7 Bring the *dashi* to the boil, season with a little salt to taste and ladle over the ingredients in each bowl, taking care not to disturb the arrangement.

8 Float a few slivers of *yuzu* on each bowl and serve immediately.

RAW FISH
Sashimi

The first item on the menu is always *sashimi*, the highlight of the meal and the pinnacle of the Japanese chef's art. It is served before the other dishes so that the expectant diners can savor each delicate morsel. Its subtle taste and texture are far removed from any Western fears of fishiness.

The fish for *sashimi* must be of impeccable quality and freshness; in many restaurants the fish is swimming in an aquarium until the last minute, and only local and seasonal fish are fresh enough to be served raw. The taste and texture of frozen fish are quite inferior. Again, only the best parts of the fish are used, and the different parts of the fish vary radically in taste.

The raw fish is always cut and arranged with great care and consummate artistry, for the *presentation* of *sashimi* is of the utmost importance. Professional chefs spend many years learning how to transform raw fish into a visual delight. The fish is garnished with a variety of condiments such as *daikon* radish, ginger root and *wasabi* horseradish, which serve as decoration as well as enhancing the flavor of the fish. *Sashimi* is always served with soy sauce or dipping sauce, into which the condiments are mixed. In spite of the mystique surrounding *sashimi*, it is easy to prepare at home. Any fish which is of good quality and absolutely fresh can be served as *sashimi*.

CHOOSING AND CUTTING FISH FOR SASHIMI

The art of cutting *sashimi* is one which most Japanese cooks prefer to leave to the professionals, buying their *sashimi* ready-cut and already beautifully arranged. But in fact the basic cutting techniques are not difficult to master.

Choosing fish for sashimi
Choose the best and freshest fish for *sashimi*. Check that the eyes are clear, the gills red, the scales firm, and the belly elastic — and that the fish has no smell. Use any fresh local fish for *sashimi;* fresh trout from a trout farm and fresh salmon are particularly prized by Japanese chefs in the West.

Preparing fish for slicing

1 Scale and gut the fish and perform Three Piece Filleting (*see* page 35). The two boneless fillets, the best part of the fish, will be used for *sashimi;* the remainder of the fish may be used in another recipe.

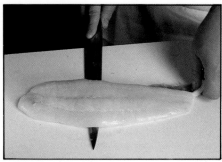

2 To skin the fillet, lay the fillet skin-side down on a damp cutting board with the tail nearest you. Holding the tail, slide a sharp long-bladed knife between the skin and the flesh, cutting as close to the skin as possible.

3 Trim the fillet into an even rectangular shape. Some kinds of fish are sold ready filleted and cut into *sashimi* lengths, and need only to be sliced.

Thick-sliced sashimi
(hira zukuri)

Use a very sharp thin-bladed knife — or even better a special *sashimi* knife — for slicing *sashimi*.

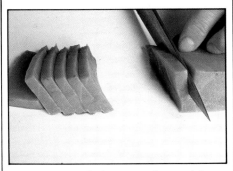

This slicing technique may be used for any fish. Lay the skinned fillet skin-side up on a cutting board, and cut straight downwards firmly and neatly into ¹/₃in slices.

The fish may be cut as thin as ¹/₄in. Arrange five or six slices on each individual plate, and garnish with thread-cut *daikon* radish (*see* page 76), parsley and *wasabi* horseradish. Serve with soy sauce to dip.

Thin-sliced sashimi
(usu zukuri)

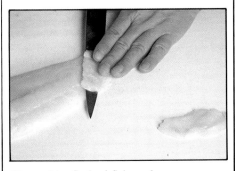

Firm white fleshed fish such as sea trout, sea bass and sole are usually cut into paper-thin slices.

Holding the fish with your fingers, cut off paper-thin slices with the edge of the knife almost horizontal. As you cut off the slices, arrange them on a plate in a rosette, overlapping the edges slightly. Garnish with finely sliced scallion and red maple radish (*see* page 77), and serve with *ponzu* sauce (*see* page 77).

DECORATIVE CUTTING TECHNIQUES

Once you have discovered the delights of raw fish, and how simple it is to prepare your own, you may wish to try some more complex cutting techniques. Raw fish is the material from which the *sashimi* chef creates a work of visual art, using the shapes and subtle colors of the fish to make an intricate, multi-colored design.

SQUID ROLLED WITH SCALLIONS AND NORI
(Ika naruto maki)

Nori seaweed and scallions give contrasting taste and texture to the squid, as well as resulting in a spectacular green and white pinwheel.

INGREDIENTS (Serves 2)
1 piece squid, 5in long
1 sheet <u>nori</u> seaweed, 7in square
¹/₂ bunch of scallions, washed, trimmed and patted dry

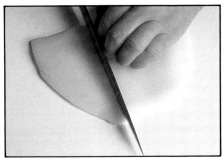

1 Clean and skin the squid. Score the outside (the shiny, smooth side) of the squid with closely-spaced, lengthways cuts, ¹/₈in deep.

2 Lightly toast the *nori* and lay over the squid; trim to fit. Arrange the bunch of scallions, alternating heads and tails, in a row along one side of the squid.

3 Roll the squid around the scallions and *nori* very firmly. Holding the roll with the seam downward, slice into ³/₈-¹/₂in slices. Serve three or four slices on individual plates, or use as part of a mixed *sashimi* dish.

TUNA ROSE
(*Magoro no bara*)

Most decorative *sashimi* arrangements include at least one "rose" made from paper-thin slices of fish. It presents an astonishing, though actually quite simple, triumph of *sashimi* art.

INGREDIENTS (Makes 1 rose)
fresh raw tuna slice

1 Cut a long, even, triangular section from the fish. With the knife at a 45° angle, cut tapering slices.

2 Carefully wrap the slices around each other to form a rose. Use fresh rose leaves to complete the illusion.

MIXED SASHIMI
(*Moriawase*)

For a feast or special occasion, the chef will be called upon to create a magnificent display of mixed *sashimi*. The centerpiece may be a whole fish, the choicest portions removed, neatly sliced and laid out on a fine wooden platter. There is no need to attempt to imitate this creation exactly: using raw fish as your palate, bring together all the *sashimi* cutting techniques of the last few pages to create your own work of art.

INGREDIENTS (Serves 4-6)
1½–2lb fresh raw fish (yellowtail
  sea bass, salmon, squid, tuna, etc)
1 cup thread-cut <u>daikon</u> radish
1 lemon, washed, dried and thinly sliced
3-4 sprigs parsley, washed and patted dry
¼ cucumber, finely sliced
2 Tbsp grated <u>wasabi</u>, or <u>wasabi</u>
  paste
soy sauce or dipping sauce (see page 76).

1 Clean, fillet and slice the fish into thick or thin slices, depending on the variety of fish. Make some decorative squid rolls and tuna roses (*see* previous recipes). Prepare garnishes, condiments and dipping sauce. Put out small individual bowls for dipping.

2 Arrange a bed of thread-cut *daikon* on a tray or attractive platter, and carefully set the *sashimi* on it. Arrange it decoratively.

3 Use the garnishes to fill the display, taking care not to disturb the fish. Add a fresh green leaf to complete the display. Serve immediately.

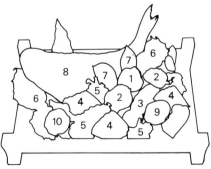

ABOVE *Mixed* <u>sashimi</u> *arranged on a wooden tray is a fine demonstration of the chef's art. (1) Squid "rose". (2) Salmon "roses". (3) Squid rolls. (4) Tuna, thick sliced. (5) Parsley. (6) Thread-cut* <u>daikon</u> *radish. (7) Decorative leaves. (8) Whole sea bass, garnished with lemon slices. (9) Lemon slices sandwiched between thin slices of squid. (10) Raw squid around a single quail's egg.*

GARNISHES, CONDIMENTS AND SAUCES FOR SASHIMI

Various garnishes, condiments and sauces are traditionally served to enhance the natural flavor of raw fish.

Garnishes
The most common accompaniment for *sashimi* is thread-cut *daikon* radish. It provides an attractive background for the fish as well as a refreshingly crisp flavor, and helps to counteract the richness of the fish. Shredded carrot and cucumber, parsley and slices of lemon are also popular garnishes.

Condiments
Sashimi would not be *sashimi* without the sudden sharp tang of *wasabi* horseradish to bring tears to the eyes. Freshly grated ginger root, red maple radish (*see* page 77) and rinsed, paper-thin leek slices (*see* "Cutting techniques", page 41) are also popular.

Dipping sauces
A variety of different dipping sauces are used with *sashimi*. These depend, not only on the type of fish, but even on the thickness of the slice. Plain soy sauce is often served, or is flavored to form a dipping sauce. With very thin slices of *sashimi*, light lemony *ponzu* sauce (*see* page 77) is preferred.

THREAD-CUT DAIKON RADISH (*kaminari*)

1 Peel the *daikon* radish into a long continuous sheet (*see* "sheet paring", page 41).

2 Cut the sheet into 8in lengths and cut the stack crosswise into fine shreds.

WASABI HORSERADISH

Wasabi can be bought ready-made in tubes and in powder form to be mixed upon like mustard. But the most delicious (and sharp) *wasabi* is freshly grated. Scrape and trim the wasabi root and grate with a circular motion on a fine-toothed grater. Form into cones to serve.

TOSA SOY SAUCE
(*Tosa joyu*)

Tosa is the old name for the southern part of Shikoku island, where the best bonito is to be found. In this popular sauce, bonito provides additional flavoring for the soy sauce. It is suitable for any fish.

INGREDIENTS
2 Tbsp sake
3 Tbsp mirin
1 piece kombu seaweed, 2in square
3 Tbsp tamari soy sauce
1 cup dark soy sauce.
1 Tbsp dried bonito flakes

1 Combine all the ingredients in a bowl and set aside in a cool place for 24 hours.

2 Strain through cheesecloth into a jar, and store in a cool, dark place. It is best to wait for at least one month for the flavor to develop — Tosa soy sauce is said to be at its best after 6 months to a year. In a cool dark place it keeps for 2 to 3 years.

RED MAPLE RADISH
(*Momiji oroshi*)

Dried chilies grated with *daikon* radish give it tang and a red color reminiscent of fall maple leaves. This popular condiment is used to accompany a wide variety of dishes.

INGREDIENTS
2in piece daikon radish
3 dried red chilies

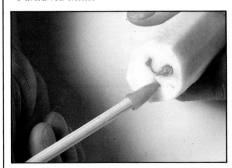

1 Peel the *daikon* radish and make three holes in one end with a **chopstick. Seed the chilies and push** them into the holes in the radish.

2 Grate the *daikon* and chilies together with a Japanese grater or a fine-toothed grater. Collect the grated mixture in a piece of cheesecloth and squeeze out as much liquid as possible. Shape into small mounds and arrange on the side of the serving dish.

PONZU SAUCE

This sauce is used for a wide variety of dishes, including *sashimi* and one pot dishes. It can be bought ready-made, but it is much more delicious—and very simple—to make your own. Make a large quantity and keep in the refrigerator to be used as required.

INGREDIENTS
1¼ cups lemon juice
1¼ cups soy sauce
3 Tbsp mirin
3 Tbsp sake
1 piece kombu seaweed 4in sq
1 Tbsp dried bonito flakes

Combine the ingredients and leave for 24 hours. Strain through cheesecloth into a jar and refrigerate. Use as required. Keeps for up to 3 months.

SIMMERED DISHES
Nimono

Whether you dine in style at a Japanese restaurant or are fortunate enough to taste home cooking, you are bound to be served at least one simmered dish. It will arrive before you as small portions of meat, fish or vegetables, served up with a little of the seasoned stock in which they are simmered. Subtle variations in the flavorings of the simmering stock result in a wide range of simmered dishes — from large one-pot dishes which are nearly a complete meal in themselves, to small side dishes of fish or vegetables.

Practically any food is suitable for simmering. The meat, fish or vegetable is first parboiled — or sometimes fried — and then simmered in a seasoned stock. The simmering stock is based on *dashi*, flavored with soy sauce, *mirin*, *sake* or *miso* in varying combinations, selected to suit the particular food to be simmered. It can range from delicate stocks of *dashi* and soy sauce to rich *miso*-based stocks. The simmering process is intended to impart flavor rather than to cook the food, and simmering times are usually quite short. Simmered foods are well-cooked but never over-cooked. Foods are frequently cooled in their simmering stock so that they can absorb even more of the flavor, and a little of the simmering stock is usually poured over the dish before serving. Japanese cooks usually use a wooden drop lid (*see* "Utensils") for simmering, to ensure that foods are completely submerged in the simmering liquid and will cook evenly.

BRAISED BEEF WITH BROCCOLI
(Gyuniku to broccoli no itame-ni)

This dish is a meeting of East and West. In it, Western ingredients such as broccoli, mushrooms and garlic — which have only recently become a part of Japanese cooking — are used to prepare a traditional Japanese-style dish. In Japan beef is sold ready-cut into paper-thin slices.

INGREDIENTS (Serves 4)
7oz sirloin of beef, thinly sliced
11oz broccoli
4oz button mushrooms
2 cloves garlic
2 Tbsp vegetable oil
1 Tbsp each sake, rice vinegar, sesame oil, water and sugar
2 tsp cornstarch

1 With a sharp knife, cut the beef into small even chunks. Wash and trim the broccoli and divide into florettes. Wipe and trim the mushrooms and halve them. Peel the garlic and slice finely.

2 Heat the oil in a large saucepan over medium heat. Add the garlic and fry for a few minutes to flavor the oil.

3 Add the mushrooms and sauté lightly. Stir in the broccoli and beef and sauté to brown the beef. Add the remaining ingredients and bring to a boil.

4 Cover with a drop lid and simmer over medium heat for 5 minutes until the beef is cooked, occasionally ladling the sauce over the beef.

5 Arrange in small deep serving bowls to serve, and ladle over a little of the stock.

SIMMERED PORK NAGASAKI-STYLE
(Buta no kaku-ni)

On the streets of Nagasaki, visitors from East and West have mingled for many centuries with the Japanese. Thus, the inhabitants of Nagasaki — unlike those of the rest of Japan — have absorbed many influences from foreign cultures. It was in Nagasaki that the first meat dishes were introduced, contravening the Buddhist law that forbids the eating of meat. This rich pork dish is usually prepared over two days. Fortunately it keeps well, and can be prepared in some quantity.

INGREDIENTS (Serves 4-6)
2¹/₄lbs pork shoulder
2¹/₂ cups water
2 x 3in piece fresh ginger, peeled
*   and crushed*
2¹/₂ cups Dashi II
4 Tbsp sugar
5-6 Tbsp dark soy sauce
1 cup sake
1 Tbsp mirin
mustard

1 Chop the pork into manageable pieces. Place them in a steamer and steam for 30 minutes.

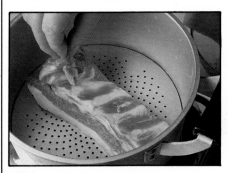

2 Remove the pork from the steamer and place in a large saucepan. Cover with the water and add the ginger.

3 Bring to a boil, skim the surface carefully, and cover with a drop lid. Simmer over lowest possible heat for at least 2 hours, topping up the water if necessary, until the pork is very tender.

4 Drain the pork, discarding the cooking water and ginger. Rinse well and refrigerate for at least 3 hours, preferably overnight.

5 An hour before you are ready to cook the pork, remove it from the refrigerator and allow it to come to room temperature.

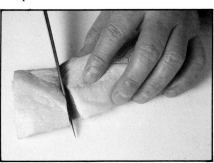

6 Cut the pork into small 1¹/₄ x 2³/₈in chunks.

7 In a dry frying pan, sauté the pork to brown it lightly.
Transfer the browned pork to a saucepan.

8 Ladle the *dashi* over the pork. Add the sugar, soy sauce, *sake* and *mirin.* Bring to a rapid boil, reduce the heat, cover with a drop lid and simmer for 30 to 40 minutes, until the simmering stock is considerably reduced.

9 Arrange a few pieces of pork on each serving dish and ladle a little of the thickened simmering stock over them. Serve with a dab of mustard.

CHICKEN SIMMERED CHIKUZEN STYLE (*Chizuken-ni*)

Chikuzen is the old name for Fukuoka Prefecture in northern Kyushu. It is from here that ferries ply their way back and forth to Korea and the Chinese mainland. Over the centuries they have brought back with them mainland influenced cooking methods, producing a cosmopolitain cuisine rather different from that of the rest of Japan. In this hearty dish, the vegetables and chicken are first stir-fried before being simmered in a little highly flavored stock, a technique very similar to that used in neighboring China.

INGREDIENTS (Serves 4)
10oz boned chicken, with skin
4 fresh shiitake or standard mushrooms,
*   wiped*
2 medium carrots
1¼ cups fresh or canned bamboo shoots
4 small potatoes, scrubbed
1 cake konnyaku (arum root)
1-2 Tbsp vegetable oil
1 cup Dashi II
2 Tbsp sugar
2 Tbsp mirin
3 Tbsp light soy sauce
2oz snow peas

1 Cut the chicken into ¾in cubes. Wash and trim the vegetables and cut into small chunks, perhaps using decorative cutting techniques. Knead the *konnyaku* with a little salt; rinse, pat dry, and tear into small pieces.

2 For the best flavor, the vegetables should be parboiled separately in lightly salted water, rinsed and drained. Heat the oil in a large saucepan over high heat.

3 Drop the chicken pieces into the oil and stir-fry to coat in oil. Add the carrots and *konnyaku,* and then the mushrooms, bamboo shoots and potatoes, in that order.

4 Stir-fry for 3 minutes, until the chicken and vegetables are lightly cooked and evenly coated with oil. Ladle the *dashi* over them, add the sugar, *mirin* and soy sauce, and bring to a boil.

5 Cover with a drop lid and simmer for 15 minutes, until the simmering stock is glossy and reduced by one-third.

6 Trim the snow peas and slice diagonally into 1in slices. Parboil in lightly salted water, and add to the chicken and vegetables just before serving.

7 Serve hot or at room temperature in individual bowls, arranging the vegetables attractively. Garnish with cress or baby parsley.

EGGPLANTS SAUTEED AND SIMMERED
(*Nasu itame-ni*)

During the heavy humidity of the summer months in Japan, eggplants are much in demand; their capacity to absorb oil is supposed to make them the ideal summer food. They are also popular for their attractive color and shape, and there are many different ways of cooking them. They are usually lightly scored and soaked in salted water, or blanched to remove bitterness, before further cooking.

INGREDIENTS (Serves 4)
2 small eggplants (1lb)
2 Tbsp vegetable oil
1¾ cups Dashi II
1 Tbsp sugar
4 Tbsp dark soy sauce
1 tsp dried bonito flakes

1 Wash and trim the eggplants. Halve lengthways and score the skin finely so that the bitter juices can drain away. Cut the eggplant into 1in slices.

2 Place the eggplant slices in a strainer and blanch with boiling water to remove the bitter juices. Cover with a light weight — such as a chopping board — and set aside for 20 minutes to drain. Rinse and pat dry.

3 In a frying pan, heat the vegetable oil and sauté the eggplants over medium heat for 7 minutes until they are tender.

4 Pour in the *dashi,* stir, and add the sugar and soy sauce. Cover with a drop lid and simmer for 10 minutes until the simmering liquid is reduced.

5 Serve individual portions in small bowls and garnish with dried bonito flakes.

ABOVE *Eggplants sautéed and simmered is a rich summer dish.*

EGGPLANTS SIMMERED IN MISO
(*Nasu no miso-ni*)

Miso makes a fine accompaniment for simmered vegetables, and goes particularly well with the richness of eggplant. In this dish, the eggplant is first fried to seal the flavor and then simmered. The dark tones of the vegetable look striking in a light-colored bowl.

INGREDIENTS (Serves 4)
2 small eggplants (about 1lb)
vegetable oil
1/2 cup Dashi II
3 Tbsp red miso
3 Tbsp sugar
1 scallion or young leek

1 Wash and trim the eggplants. Halve lengthways, and score the skin with fairly deep diagonal cuts, about 1/2in apart.

2 In a frying pan, heat a little vegetable oil and sauté the eggplants over medium heat until they are translucent. Add the *dashi,* cover with a drop lid, and simmer over very low heat for 5 minutes.

3 Combine the *miso* and sugar in a small bowl. Add a little of the hot stock and mix well with a whisk to dissolve the *miso.*

4 Add this thick sauce to the eggplants and continue to simmer over low heat until the eggplants are well cooked.

5 Serve mounded in the center of deep light-colored dishes. Slice a scallion or young leek into very fine rings and scatter over the eggplant as a garnish.

MACKEREL SIMMERED IN MISO
(Saba no miso-ni)

Miso flavored with ginger makes a savory and piquant simmering stock, which sets off the richness of mackerel. After cooking, the mackerel is usually left to cool in the stock to allow the flavors to penetrate. This method of cooking is suitable for any round-bodied oily fish.

INGREDIENTS *(Serves 4)*
4 mackerel fillets, skin intact
salt
1oz fresh ginger
1¼ cups Dashi II
2 Tbsp sake
5 Tbsp red miso
¼ cup sugar

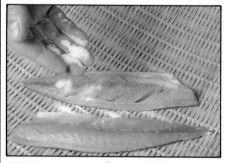

1 Rinse the fillets in cold water and pat dry. Arrange the fillets on a strainer and sprinkle with 2 Tbsp salt; set aside to drain for at least 1 hour.

2 With a sharp knife, cut each fillet into three or four pieces. Bring plenty of water to a rolling boil. To blanch the fillets, place them in a strainer and immerse in boiling water for a few minutes. Remove, drain and set aside.

3 Peel half of the ginger and slice into paper-thin slices. Arrange the fillets in a single layer in a frying pan or large skillet.

4 Pour the *dashi* and *sake* over the fillets, add the ginger slices and bring to a simmer. Cover with a drop lid and simmer over very low heat until the fillets are firm and white.

5 Combine the *miso* and sugar in a small bowl. Add a little of the hot stock and mix well with a whisk to dissolve the *miso*. Add the *miso* mixture to the simmering mackerel liquid, and stir.

6 Cover with the drop lid and continue to simmer, occasionally spooning the *miso* stock over the fish, until the stock becomes thick and glossy. Remove the saucepan from the heat and set aside to allow the mackerel to cool in the stock.

7 Peel and shred the remaining ginger and put into a little water to soak. Remove the mackerel fillets from the *miso* stock and arrange in individual serving bowls. Ladle the *miso* stock over the fillets, garnish with ginger shreads and serve.

MACKEREL SIMMERED IN SAKE
(Saba no nitsuke)

When the technique of *sake* simmering is applied to round-bodied oily fish such as mackerel, a richer, more concentrated, simmering stock is used to set off the strong flavor.

INGREDIENTS (Serves 4)
4 mackerel fillets, about 3oz each
a pinch of salt
1 cup sake
½ cup mirin
¼ cup dark soy sauce
2 Tbsp shredded fresh ginger

1 Rinse the fillets in cold water and pat dry. Arrange the fillets on a strainer and sprinkle with a little salt; set aside to drain for at least 1 hour. Rinse in cold water and pat dry.

2 With a sharp knife, cut each fillet into three or four pieces. In a large saucepan bring the *sake* to a simmer. Arrange the fish in a single layer in the simmering *sake*, dark side uppermost, and bring the *sake* rapidly back to a boil. This process blanches the mackerel.

3 Add the remaining ingredients, bring to a boil and carefully skim the surface. Cover with a drop lid and cook over high heat for about 10 minutes until the flesh is tender and the stock is reduced by two-thirds.

4 Turn off the heat and leave the fish in the hot stock before serving. After a few minutes, carefully remove the fish from the stock with a slotted spatula and arrange the fillets in individual bowls. Garnish with the ginger and spoon the stock over the fish.

SOLE SIMMERED IN SAKE
(*Karei nitsuke*)

Sole simmered in a rich stock based on *sake* makes a delicious winter entrée. In summer the same dish may be served cold; the chilled simmering stock forms a savory aspic. In true Japanese style, small whole sole is simmered and carefully served with the head pointing to the left. Western sole tends to be larger than those available in Japan, and should be first divided into portions.

INGREDIENTS (Serves 4)
4 3oz fillets of sole
salt
¹/₃oz fresh ginger
1 cup <u>Dashi II</u>
4 Tbsp <u>sake</u>
4 Tbsp dark soy sauce
4 Tbsp <u>mirin</u>
1 tsp salt
4in piece dried <u>wakame</u> *seaweed,*
    reconstituted (see page 39)

1 Lay the fish fillets on a cutting surface with the dark side uppermost. With a sharp knife make a shallow cross, about ¹/₄in deep, in the top of each fillet, to allow the fish to absorb the flavor of the simmering liquid more thoroughly.

2 Arrange the fillets on a strainer and sprinkle with a little salt; set aside to drain for at least 1 hour. Rinse in cold water and pat dry. Peel the ginger and slice thinly.

3 Combine the *dashi, sake,* soy sauce, *mirin* and salt in a large saucepan and bring to a boil. Arrange the fish in a single layer in the simmering stock, with the dark side on top.

4 Add the ginger. Return to a boil, carefully skim the surface, cover with a drop lid, and cook over medium heat, occasionally ladling the simmering stock over the fish pieces, until the stock is reduced by half.

5 Cut the reconstituted *wakame* into 1in pieces and add to the simmering stock. Continue to simmer for a few more minutes until the stock is thick and much reduced. Turn off the heat and leave the fish for a few minutes in the hot stock before serving.

6 With a slotted spatula, remove the fish. Arrange in individual bowls and distribute the *wakame* and ginger evenly. Pour over a little of the simmering stock and serve.

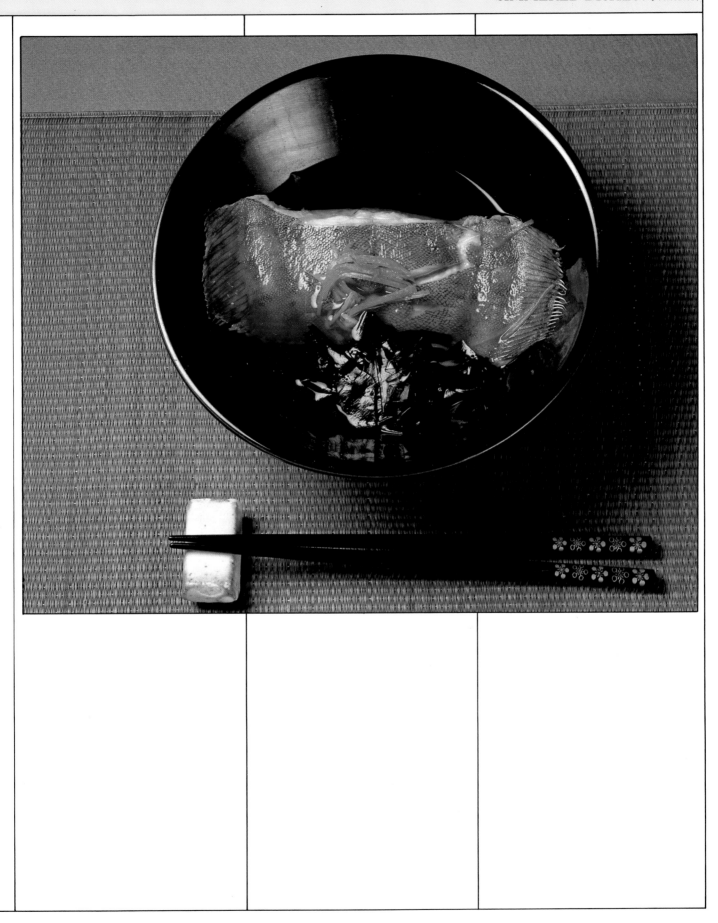

CRAB AND NAPA CABBAGE SIMMERED YOSHINO STYLE
(Kani to hakusai no yoshino-ni)

This dish combines crab meat with lightly boiled napa cabbage leaves in a thickened sauce. The simmering sauce is traditionally thickened with *kuzu*, which gives a particularly light and translucent finish. It is also reputed to have great medicinal qualities. Yoshino *kuzu* is said to be the best of all. After adding *kuzu*, the sauce needs to be continually stirred until it thickens, to prevent lumpiness. Arrowroot or cornstarch are acceptable alternatives for *kuzu*.

INGREDIENTS (Serves 4)
6 leaves napa cabbage
2½ cups Dashi II
2 tsp salt
1 tsp light soy sauce
1 Tbsp mirin
1 Tbsp sake
¾ cup fresh crab meat (or 5oz canned crab meat)
2 Tbsp kuzu, arrowroot or cornstarch

1 Wash the Chinese cabbage leaves and parboil in plenty of lightly salted water for 3 minutes. Drain and cut into 2in pieces.

2 Put the *dashi* into a medium size saucepan and bring to a simmer. Add the napa cabbage, and stir in the salt, soy sauce, *mirin* and *sake*.

3 Flake the crab meat and add to the simmering stock. Cover with a drop lid and simmer for 3 minutes.

4 Dissolve the *kuzu* in ½ cup cold water, and pour gradually into the simmering stock, stirring continuously. Continue to stir over very low heat until the sauce thickens.

5 Remove the napa cabbage and crab meat and arrange in small, deep bowls; ladle over the thickened sauce and serve hot.

GOLDEN PRAWNS
(Ebi no kimi-ni)

Japanese prawns are large and succulent
and a favorite throughout the country. In
the egg yolk simmering technique, the
prawns are dredged in cornstarch and
then dipped into the yolk to form a
golden coating before simmering in a
seasoned stock. Garnished with potatoes
and bright green beans, the golden
prawns make a colorful dish. This
simmering technique may also be used
with shrimps, scallops and chicken.

INGREDIENTS (Serves 4)
8 large prawns or jumbo shrimp
8 small potatoes (about 12oz)
2½ cups <u>*Dashi II*</u>
3 Tbsp <u>*sake*</u>
6 Tbsp <u>*mirin*</u>
4 Tbsp light soy sauce
6oz green beans
3 Tbsp cornstarch
3 egg yolks
yuzu or lemon peel (optional)

1 Shell and devein the prawns,
leaving the tail intact. Slit open the
back of the prawn. Score the back of
each prawn and press it out flat.

2 Peel and trim the potatoes and cut
into small equal size balls. Parboil
in lightly salted water covered with a
drop lid until just tender. Drain and
refresh in cold water.

3 Combine the *dashi, sake, mirin*
and soy sauce in a saucepan; add
the potatoes and bring to a boil. Remove
from heat and set aside, so that the
potatoes cool in the simmering stock and
absorb the flavor.

4 Trim the beans and cut diagonally
into 2in pieces. Parboil in lightly
salted water until the beans are just
tender. Drain and refresh immediately in
cold water to prevent further cooking.

5 Bring the simmering stock to a
simmer. Holding the prepared
prawns by the tail, brush each prawn
with cornstarch to make an even coating.

6 Separate the egg yolks into a small
bowl, and beat until frothy.
Holding the bowl of egg yolks over the
simmering stock, dip the prawns into the
egg yolk, holding each prawn by the tail.

7 Carefully lay the prawns in the
stock and simmer gently,
uncovered, until the egg is set and the
tails are bright pink. The egg yolk
coating will puff up a little as the prawns
cook. Put the beans into the simmering
stock to reheat.

8 Arrange the prawns against the potatoes in small serving bowls and place the beans in front. Ladle over the simmering stock. This dish may be garnished with *yuzu* or lemon peel.

GRILLED DISHES
Yakimono

The process of grilling harks back to man's hunting days, when freshly-caught fish or animals were cooked directly over an open fire. The simplest cooking methods are still preferred in Japan, and grilling, together with shallow frying—indirect grilling—is one of the most popular. Every Japanese meal includes at least one grilled dish, usually fish or chicken.

Grilling is simple in theory but difficult to perform to perfection. The food must be carefully skewered so that it keeps its shape, and grilled over heat carefully adjusted to ensure that the skin quickly crisps while the flesh remains succulent and tender. Charcoal, which gives the strongest heat, is ideal. Professional cooks in Japan use a special smokeless charcoal, but an ordinary gas flame grill or broiler is perfectly adequate.

Food to be grilled or broiled is often first salted or marinated in a mixture of *sake,* soy sauce and *mirin.* In order to ensure that the finished dish looks as attractive as possible, the front of the fish, the part that will be seen, is always grilled or broiled first, and the fish is turned only once, when it is more than half done, and removed from the fire just before it is completely cooked. It is always served facing to the left, the head a little to the front, with perhaps a small mound of grated *daikon* radish.

SKEWERING

Before grilling, the fish or meat must be threaded onto skewers to support it when it is set over the fire. As with so many things in Japan, this simple process has been turned into quite an art. The Japanese have developed a variety of skewering methods which ensure that the food holds its shape during cooking.

When it is served, the skewer holes should be invisible, the fish looking as if it has just leapt out of the sea. Stainless steel skewers in a variety of lengths are most commonly used, together with bamboo skewers which are preferred for a few specific dishes.

Before skewering, the food needs to be carefully washed and cut into pieces of the appropriate size and shape.

Long skewering
(Tate gushi)

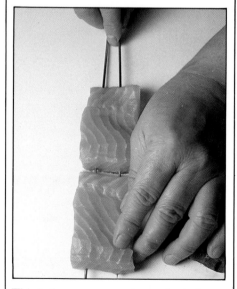

This is the most common method of skewering. Resting your left hand on the fish, slide the skewers along the grain of the fish. Take care that the skewers do not pierce the surface.

One-tuck skewering
(Kata zuma ori)

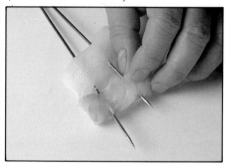

This skewering method is named after the habit of tucking up one's encumbering kimono when working and is used mainly for thin fillets. Gently roll up one end of the fillet and secure it with a skewer.

Two-tuck skewering
(Ryo zuma ori)

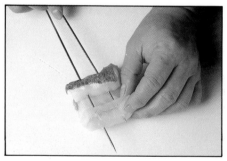

Repeat the above procedure with both ends of the fillet. This skewering technique gives added body to thin fillets and ensures that the inside remains soft and tender during cooking.

Skewering a whole fish
(Ayu sugata yaki)

see opposite

Stitch skewering (*Nui gushi*)

Thin slabs of squid tend to shrink and warp during grilling, and need to be stretched out on the skewers.

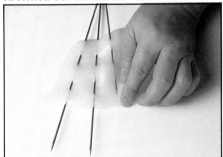

Resting one hand on the fish, thread several skewers in and out along the squid like stitches, forming a fan shape. Take care that the skewers do not pierce the top of the squid.

Insert one short skewer diagonally to secure the shape. No skewers should be visible on the surface of the fish.

Skewering rolled shrimps

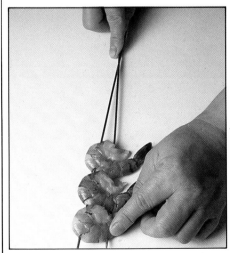

Gently curl two or three shrimps and slide two skewers through to hold the shape.

ABOVE *An array of skewered foods ready to be grilled.*

SALT-GRILLED FISH (*Ayu sugata yaki*)

The *pièce de résistance* among grilled foods is a whole fish—simply skewered so that it retains its shape—which is salted and grilled. Eaten hot off the grill, the skin crisp and the flesh tender, salt-grilled fish is a true delicacy, which needs simply to be served with a squeeze of lemon or a drop of soy sauce. Any small to medium fish may be prepared in this way. Grilling over charcoal gives the best flavor, but of course you can salt grill on any type of grill or broiler.

INGREDIENTS (Serves 4)
4 sweetfish (ayu), mackerel, trout or other
   medium size fish
salt
lemon wedges
soy sauce
4 pickled ginger shoots

1 Scale and gut the fish (*see* page 34), leaving head and tail intact.

2 Hold the fish with the head pointing to the right, so that the "back" of the fish is facing you, and thread one or two skewers through the fish, making sure that the skewers do not pierce the "front" of the fish. Prick the skin a few times with a needle.

3 Take a pinch of salt and rub it into the tail and fins, so that they are heavily coated with salt. This is known as "cosmetic" salting, and prevents the tail and fins from burning.

4 Lightly salt the entire fish. Grill over high heat, grilling the front of the fish first and turning only once.

5 Remove the skewers and arrange fish facing to the left, with the head slightly toward the front. Garnish with lemon wedges or soy sauce and pickled red ginger shoots.

GRILLED CHICKEN (*Yakitori*)

After a hard day at the office, many a Japanese businessman retires to a *yakitori* restaurant, where the chefs grill up skewerfuls of succulent chicken morsels over a hot charcoal grill. *Yakitori* is one of the classic Japanese dishes, enjoyed throughout Japan. The chicken thigh is the most commonly used, but the liver and wings may also feature. Grilled chicken skin is considered to be a great delicacy. Bamboo skewers are used for *yakitori*, and should be carefully washed and left to dry after use.

INGREDIENTS (Serves 4)
2¼lbs boned chicken thigh
4 young leeks, washed and trimmed

YAKITORI SAUCE:
1¾ cups dark soy sauce
1 cup chicken stock
1 cup sake
½ cup sugar
½ cup mirin

1 Combine the *yakitori* sauce ingredients in a saucepan. Bring it to a boil, and simmer gently for 5 minutes. Remove from the heat and cool to room temperature. Transfer the sauce to a deep jar. (This amount of *yakitori* sauce can be used for several meals, and should be stored tightly sealed in the refrigerator.)

2 Cut the chicken into 1in pieces, and cut the leeks into 1½in lengths. Thread the chicken and leeks alternately onto bamboo skewers.

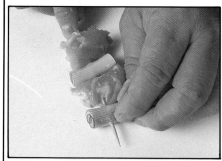

3 Grill over the hottest flame, turning frequently to avoid burning. When the juices begin to drip, dip the skewered chicken into the sauce and return to the grill. Repeat this several times until the chicken is lightly cooked. Be careful not to overcook the chicken; it should remain moist.

4 Serve the chicken piping hot, on the skewers, and spoon over a little of the *yakitori* sauce. Traditionally, *yakitori* is sprinkled with a little dash of Seven spice pepper, and eaten with the fingers straight from the skewer.

SALT-GRILLED CHICKEN (*Shio yakitori*)

Salt grilling accentuates the succulent taste of chicken.

INGREDIENTS (Serves 4)
8 small boned chicken thighs, skin intact
2 Tbsp sake
salt
lemon wedges

1 Sprinkle the chicken thighs with *sake* and leave to stand for 5 to 10 minutes to tenderize. Thread onto skewers.

2 Sprinkle both sides liberally with salt.

3 Grill over a hot flame for 10 minutes, turning occasionally, until the skin is golden and the flesh is cooked but still moist. Garnish with lemon wedges. Serve hot or at room temperature.

ABOVE *Three versions of the ever-popular* <u>*yakitori:*</u> *(top right) grilled chicken* (<u>*yakitori*</u>) *garnished with parsley; (center) salt-grilled chicken* (<u>*shio yakitori*</u>) *garnished with parsley and lemon; (bottom right) grilled chicken with red and white miso toppings* (<u>*miso yakitori*</u>) *garnished with parsley.*

GRILLED CHICKEN WITH MISO
(*Miso yakitori*)

In this version of *yakitori*, the chicken is brushed with a rich sweet *miso* topping.

INGREDIENTS (Serves 4)
2¼lbs boned chicken thigh
4 young leeks, washed and trimmed

MISO TOPPING
½ cup <u>miso</u>
1½ Tbsp sugar
3 Tbsp <u>sake</u>
2 Tbsp <u>mirin</u>

1 Combine the *miso* topping ingredients in a saucepan. Heat until the sugar dissolves and set aside. (This amount of *miso* topping can be used for several meals.)

2 Cut the chicken into 1in pieces and cut the leeks into 1½in lengths. Thread the chicken and leeks alternately onto bamboo skewers. Grill over the hottest flame, turning frequently, until nearly cooked.

3 Brush evenly with *miso* topping and continue grilling. Turn the *miso* topped side towards the fire, and brush the other side with *miso* topping. Repeat this process two or three times with each skewer. Serve immediately.

ROLLED OMELET WITH PEAS
(*Dashimaki tamago*)

This light, slightly sweet rolled omelet is a great favorite in Japan, served in neat golden slices garnished with a little grated radish. Japanese cooks use a rectangular omelet pan to make a symmetrical shape, and a bamboo rolling mat to finish it, but the omelet can be made in an ordinary omelet pan and trimmed.

INGREDIENTS (Serves 4)
5 eggs
1 cup Dashi II
1 Tbsp mirin
1½ Tbsp light soy sauce
a pinch of salt
1 Tbsp peas
vegetable oil
1½ Tbsp grated daikon radish
soy sauce

1 Break the eggs into a bowl. Add *dashi, mirin,* soy sauce and salt. Mix lightly with a whisk and stir in the peas.

2 Brush the omelet pan lightly with oil, and heat over moderately high heat.

3 Pour in just enough of the egg mixture to coat the pan, tilting the pan so that the egg mixture forms an even layer.

4 As soon as the egg is set, tilt the pan and roll "top" of the omelet toward you, to form a roll at the front of the pan.

5 Push the roll to the back of the pan. Brush the pan with oil and pour in a little more of the egg mixture, lifting the roll to allow the egg mixture to flow underneath it.

6 Allow the egg mixture to set and proceed as before, tilting the pan and rolling the omelet toward you to form a roll, then pushing to the back of the pan. Repeat until all the egg mixture is used and there is a thick roll at the end of the pan.

7 Place the bamboo rolling mat over the omelet and remove the omelet from the pan; or use a slotted spatula. Roll the omelet in the bamboo mat, press gently, and leave to rest for 1 minute.

8 Unroll the omelet and slice into 1in pieces. Arrange on small serving plates. Moisten the grated *daikon* with a little soy sauce, and place a small mound on each plate to garnish.

SWEET-GLAZED BEEF
(*Gyuniku teriyaki*)

Beef is perhaps even more of a luxury in Japan than it is in the West, and tends to be reserved for special occasions. It is usually sold ready-sliced into steaks. In the *teriyaki* technique, the beef is fried and then brushed with a sweet glaze.

The *teriyaki* sauce which forms the glaze is used in many dishes. It is best to make a large quantity and store it in the refrigerator.

INGREDIENTS (Serves 4)
1¾ cups mushrooms, wiped and trimmed
2 tomatoes
¾ cup bean sprouts
⅓ cup snow peas
salt
4 sirloin steaks
vegetable oil
6 Tbsp grated apple

TERIYAKI SAUCE
1 cup soy sauce
1 cup sake
½ cup mirin
¼ cup sugar

1 Prepare the *teriyaki* sauce: combine the soy sauce, *sake, mirin* and sugar in a saucepan and stir over medium heat to dissolve the sugar. The sauce may be used immediately or cooled and refrigerated.

2 Cut a neat cross in the top of each mushroom cap. Wash the vegetables and pat dry. Halve the tomatoes, trim the bean sprouts and cut the snow peas diagonally into 1in slices. Lightly salt the steaks and set aside for 5 to 20 minutes.

3 Heat a little oil in a frying pan and sauté the vegetables for 2 or 3 minutes or until cooked but still a little crisp. Remove, drain and keep warm.

4 Drain the frying pan and add fresh oil. Heat the oil over medium to high heat, add the steaks and fry until both sides are brown.

5 Pour *teriyaki* sauce over the steaks. Add grated apple to the pan. Tilt the pan and turn the steaks so that they are well coated with sauce, and heat until the sauce begins to bubble.

6 Serve the meat and vegetables on individual plates. In Japan cast iron plates are preferred for this dish. Pour the remaining *teriyaki* sauce in the pan over the steaks and serve immediately.

SWEET GLAZED CHICKEN
(*Tori no teriyaki*)

Sweet *teriyaki* sauce makes a delicious complement for the mild taste of chicken. Serve this dish with skewered and deep-fried green peppers.

INGREDIENTS (Serves 4)
2 chicken legs and thighs, boned
vegetable oil
teriyaki sauce (see page 100)

1 Pierce the skin of the chicken with a fork to allow the sauce to penetrate. Brush a frying pan with oil and fry the chicken over high heat, turning, until well browned.

2 Remove the chicken from the heat and rinse with boiling water. Return the chicken pieces to the pan and pour over the *teriyaki* sauce. Cook until the sauce is glossy, turning the chicken so that it is well coated in sauce. Remove from heat when the sauce is well reduced and thick.

3 Cut the chicken into ½in slices, and arrange the slices on individual plates. Serve hot.

SWEET GLAZED SALMON
(Sake no teriyaki)

Sweet glazed dishes are often grilled or broiled rather than fried, to make a less rich dish. Oily fish such as salmon, tuna and mackerel are particularly suited to this treatment when served with *teriyaki* sauce. Buy fish fillets or steaks complete with skin, which becomes deliciously crisp when grilled.

INGREDIENTS (Serves 4)
4 salmon fillets
teriyaki sauce (see page 100)

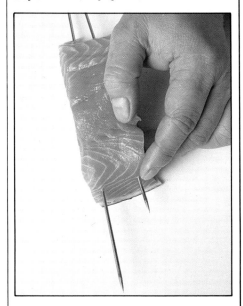

1 Cut the fillets in 1in slices, and skewer, being careful not to pierce the skin.

2 Grill the salmon over very high heat, cooking the flesh side first.

3 Turn the salmon to grill the skin-side, and brush with *teriyaki* sauce. Serve immediately, and spoon over a little more *teriyaki* sauce.

SQUID STUFFED WITH VEGETABLES
(Ika kenchin yaki)

Whole squid lend themselves to stuffing, and in this dish a characteristically Japanese stuffing is used. Squid need to be cooked over the hottest possible flame for a very short time so as not to become tough.

INGREDIENTS (Serves 4)
4 squid
1 small carrot
¼ cup peas or French beans
vegetable oil
3 eggs, beaten
salt

MISO TOPPING (*see "Grilled chicken with miso"*)

1 Gut and trim the squid and rinse well. Parboil the vegetables and chop the carrot and beans finely.

2 Brush a small pan with oil, add the vegetables and sauté lightly. Stir in the egg over low heat, and continue to stir until the egg mixture is nearly set. Remove from the heat and season to taste with a little salt.

3 Stuff each squid about half full with the vegetable mixture, and use a toothpick to close the "bag". Brush each squid with *miso* topping.

4 Grill the squid over high heat for 3–4 minutes, and serve immediately.

BEEF AND VEGETABLE ROLLS
(Gyuhire yasai maki)

A rich and colorful dish of carrot, asparagus and beans rolled in paper-thin slices of beef, and topped with a savory sauce.

INGREDIENTS (Serves 4)
1 medium carrot
4oz asparagus
4oz French beans
12oz prime beef, sliced paper-thin
cornstarch or potato flour
vegetable oil

SAUCE
1 Tbsp sugar
3 Tbsp water
1 Tbsp sake
1 Tbsp mirin
3 Tbsp soy sauce

1 Scrape the carrot and cut into long narrow strips. Trim the asparagus. Top and tail the beans.

2 Parboil the vegetables separately in lightly salted water until just tender. Drain immediately and refresh in cold water. Drain and pat dry.

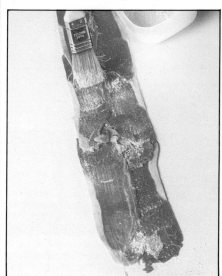

3 On a chopping board, lay half the meat slices side by side with edges overlapping to form a sheet of even width. Press the overlapping sections gently so that they stick. Brush with cornstarch.

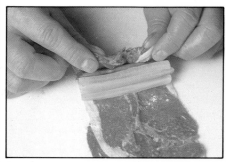

4 Lay a few strips of each vegetable at one end of the beef sheet. Roll up firmly.

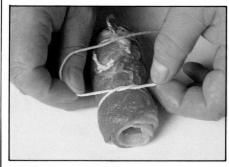

5 Tie securely with white cotton string. Repeat the process with the remaining beef and vegetables.

6 Combine the sauce ingredients in a bowl and stir well to blend.

7 Put a little oil into a frying pan and heat over high heat. Add the rolls and sauté until lightly browned.

8 Pour the sauce over the rolls and bring to a simmer. Continue to simmer over low heat for 5 minutes, until the beef is tender and well flavored.

9 To serve, cut the strings and slice the rolls into 1in rounds. Arrange on individual serving dishes and spoon over a little of the sauce.

NAMBA-STYLE BACON AND LEEK ROLLS (*Namba maki*)

Namba, now right in the center of the huge city of Osaka, was once renowned for its leeks.

INGREDIENTS (Serves 4)
8 slices Canadian bacon
cornstarch
6 young leeks
vegetable oil

1 Trim the bacon, and lay three or four slices side by side with edges overlapping to form a sheet of even width. Press the overlapping sections gently so that they stick. Brush the bacon with cornstarch.

2 Trim the leeks. Place three leeks at one end of the bacon sheet, alternating tops and tails of the leeks. Carefully roll the leeks in the bacon.

3 Tie the rolls securely with white cotton string.

4 Put a little oil into a frying pan, and heat over high heat.

5 Place the tied rolls in the pan and fry, turning, for about 7 minutes, until the bacon is cooked to taste and the leeks are tender. Repeat with the remaining bacon and leeks.

6 Remove the strings and cut the rolls into ½in slices.

ABOVE *Namba-style bacon and leek rolls neatly arranged in the center of a delicate porcelain plate, and garnished with parsley.*

TOFU TOPPED WITH SWEET MISO
(*Tofu dengaku*)

Squares of *tofu* on two-pronged bamboo skewers—grilled over charcoal and served with the sweet *miso* sauce while still sizzling—is a favorite holiday food.

INGREDIENTS (Serves 4)
White and red <u>miso</u> sauces (see page 108)
1lb <u>tofu</u>
Black and white sesame seeds, toasted

1 First drain the *tofu*: set a weight such as a chopping board or dinner plate on the *tofu* and set aside for at least 30 minutes to drain.

2 Slice the *tofu* into thick oblongs, $1/2$ x 1 x 2in. Insert a two-pronged skewer or two single bamboo skewers into each piece.

3 Grill over a hot flame for 3 minutes on each side. Spread one side with *miso* sauce and garnish with sesame seeds to complement the color.

4 Grill the *miso*-topped side for 1 or 2 minutes, until heated through and bubbling. Serve immediately.

MARINATED PORK AND LEEK ROLLS
(*Buta no negi maki*)

These pork rolls are marinated in a sweetened soy sauce and *sake* mixture and then grilled.

INGREDIENTS (Serves 4)
8 young leeks
8 paper-thin slices of pork

MARINADE
3 Tbsp <u>sake</u>
3 Tbsp sugar
1/4 cup dark soy sauce

1 Wash the leeks and trim away the green sections; put these aside to use in another dish. Roll each leek firmly in a strip of pork, and tie securely with string.

2 Mix the marinade ingredients, and pour over the rolls. Leave to marinade for 1 hour, turning occasionally. Drain, reserving the marinade for basting.

3 Thread two or three skewers through the rolls like a fan. Grill the rolls over a hot flame for 6 minutes, turning and basting with the marinade occasionally.

4 Remove the skewers, cut the strings, and slice the rolls into 1in lengths to serve.

EGGPLANT TOPPED WITH SWEET MISO
(*Nasu dengaku*)

Many temples in Japan have a small restaurant on the grounds, where weary visitors can take a rest, while enjoying a dish of vegetables or *tofu*, charcoal-grilled or fried, and topped with sweetened *miso*. This popular dish is delicious and also simple to make. In addition the contrasting colors of the *miso* sauces give it great visual appeal.

INGREDIENTS (Serves 4)
2 medium eggplants
vegetable oil

WHITE MISO SAUCE
½ cup white <u>miso</u>
1 Tbsp sugar
⅓ cup <u>mirin</u>

RED MISO SAUCE
½ cup red <u>miso</u>
1½ Tbsp sugar
⅓ cup <u>mirin</u>

White sesame seeds, toasted
Black sesame seeds or poppy seeds, toasted

1 Prepare the two *miso* sauces. Combine the ingredients for the white *miso* sauce in the top of a double boiler, and cook very gently over simmering water, stirring with a wooden spoon, until the sugar is dissolved and the sauce is the consistency of mayonnaise. Set aside. Repeat for the red *miso* sauce. (These quantities give enough *miso* sauce for several meals. The sauces will keep for 1 month.)

2 Trim the stem of the eggplants and halve lengthways. Score the eggplant flesh so that heat will penetrate more quickly.

3 Heat 2 Tbsp vegetable oil over medium heat in a frying pan, and fry the eggplants until well cooked, turning occasionally. Add more oil if necessary. Drain on paper towels.

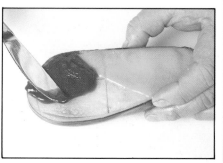

4 With a knife, spread the cut face of alternate eggplant halves with the two *miso* sauces.

5 Sprinkle a few black sesame seeds or poppy seeds on the white *miso* sauce to garnish.

6 Sprinkle a few white sesame seeds on the red *miso* sauce.

SCALLOPS IN GREEN SAUCE
(*Hotategai no midoriyaki*)

The most prized scallops are to be found off the coast of the northernmost island of Hokkaido. So fresh are these fish, taken straight from the shell, that it would be a crime to eat them any way except raw. If cooked, they are always served quite simply. In the following recipe, the scallops are served with a rich green *miso* sauce and baked in the oven, using a technique adapted from the West.

INGREDIENTS (*Serves 4*)
4–8 sea scallops
salt
vegetable oil

MISO SAUCE
5 leaves spinach
¼ cup white *miso*
2 Tbsp *mirin*
3 Tbsp water

1 Wash the scallops, pat dry and salt them lightly. Brush a shallow baking dish with oil, and arrange the scallops in it.

2 Prepare the *miso* sauce: wash the spinach leaves and pat them dry. Chop them roughly, place them in a *suribachi* or food processor and grind them to a paste. Stir in the *miso, mirin* and water. Blend to make a smooth green sauce.

3 Spread the *miso* sauce in a thick layer on the scallops. Bake for 3–4 minutes in a preheated hot oven, so that the scallops are just heated. If overcooked, the scallops will become tough.

RIGHT *Mixed grill (teppan yaki). An appetizing array of meat and vegetables grilled on the table, and served piping hot with a rich sauce and various condiments.*

MIXED GRILL
(*Teppan yaki*)

In *teppan yaki* restaurants, each table has a heated cast iron surface on which meat, fish and vegetables are fried before the customers' eyes, and served up with a variety of sauces and condiments. At home this mixed grill may be cooked at table using an electric griddle or electric frying pan.

INGREDIENTS (*Serves 4*)
4 small 4oz boneless fillets of steak
4 sea scallops
2 medium onions
2 oz mushrooms
2 oz snow peas
1 green pepper
4 prawns/jumbo shrimp, shelled and deveined
4 white fish fillets or steaks
vegetable oil

SAUCE
4 ½cups soy sauce
2 cups *mirin*
2 ½ cups *sake*
⅓ cup ginger juice
1½ Tbsp sesame oil

CONDIMENTS
grated <u>daikon</u> radish
red maple radish (see page 77)
<u>ponzu</u> vinegar (see page 77)
freshly made mustard

1 Trim the steaks. Wash the scallops and pat dry. Peel and slice the onions. Cut a cross in the top of each mushroom. Trim the snow peas. Deseed the pepper and cut lengthways into eighths. Put the sauce ingredients into a jar and shake well.

2 Set the griddle in the center of the table. Set a small bowl containing a little of the sauce at each place, and arrange bowls of each condiment on the table.

3 Heat the griddle and brush with oil. Fry the meat, shellfish, prawns, fish and vegetables—a few at a time, over medium heat—turning, until done. The diners help themselves to the various foods as they please, adding sauce and condiments to taste.

DEEP-FRIED DISHES
Agemono

I n Japan deep-frying has developed into a refined and sophisticated art, producing light, crisp dishes without a trace of oiliness. Bite size pieces of fish, meat and vegetables are cooked in a few seconds, so that all the freshness and flavor are conserved.

The secret of perfect deep-frying lies in the oil. The Japanese use only pure vegetable oil—never animal fats—adding a little sesame oil to give a nutty flavor. Oil for deep-frying can be reused a few times, but the most delicious deep-fried foods are those made with fresh oil.

Secondly, the oil must be kept at a high, even temperature. The correct temperature varies depending on the food which is being deep-fried; meat and fish need to be cooked at a higher temperature than vegetables. You can check the temperature of the oil with a deep-frying thermometer, or use the batter test. Drop a little batter or a tiny piece of bread into the hot oil; at 325°F (170°C), the usual deep-frying temperature, it will sink slightly into the oil, then rise quickly to the surface. If it sizzles on the surface of the oil without sinking, the oil temperature is about 350°F (180°C), too hot for deep frying; if it sinks to the bottom and does not rise, the oil is only about 300°F (150°C)—too low. A temperature of 315°F (160°C)—at which bread would rise gently to the surface—should be fine for vegetable deep-frying.

Always deep-fry in plenty of oil and cook only a few items at a time, so that the oil temperature remains constant. Japanese cooks deep-fry in a small heavy saucepan, fitted with a small rack, so that the oil from the cooked foods can drain back into the pan. Chopsticks—together with a skimmer to clear the oil—are the only utensils used. Deep-fried foods should always be served immediately, after being briefly drained on paper towels. They are usually served either in, or with, a delicately-flavored sauce.

DEEP-FRIED CHICKEN TATSUTA STYLE
(Toriniku tatsuta age)

Morsels of chicken marinaded in soy sauce become a rich reddish brown, reminiscent of the famed fall maple leaves of Tatsuta, near the ancient capital of Nara. Fresh ginger gives a tang to the marinade and is frequently used to accompany chicken in Japanese cooking.

INGREDIENTS (Serves 4)
1½lb boned chicken, skin attached

6 Tbsp cornstarch
vegetable oil for deep frying
1 lemon, washed, dried and quartered
4 sprigs parsley, washed and patted dry

MARINADE
4 Tbsp soy sauce
2 Tbsp sake
1 Tbsp sugar
1 Tbsp ginger juice

1 Cut the chicken into large bite-size chunks. Mix the marinade ingredients and pour over the chicken. Mix well so that the chicken is evenly covered. Set aside to marinate for 30 minutes.

2 Drain the chicken and coat with cornstarch. Wait for a few minutes so that the coating can set.

3 In a small saucepan, heat oil for deep frying to 350°F (180°C). Carefully place the chicken in the oil, a few pieces at a time, and deep-fry for about 3 minutes, until crisp and brown.

4 Remove piece by piece and drain. Arrange a few pieces of chicken on a neatly folded paper napkin. Garnish with lemon quarters and sprigs of parsley.

BREADED PORK CUTLET
(*Tonkatsu*)

Tonkatsu is one of the most popular lunchtime foods, served up daily in restaurants and homes all over Japan. With a simple salad and a dash of Worcestershire sauce, it makes a filling and delicious meal.

INGREDIENTS (Serves 4)
4 slices pork loin or tenderloin, 4–5oz each
salt and pepper
4 Tbsp flour
2 eggs, lightly beaten
2 cups homemade breadcrumbs
vegetable oil for deep frying
4 lettuce leaves
1 lemon
freshly made mustard

DIPPING SAUCE
Worcestershire sauce
ketchup
dark soy sauce
sake
freshly made mustard

1 Place each piece of loin or tenderloin between two sheets of waxed paper. Pound until flattened into a thin cutlet. Trim the cutlets and score the edges in a few places to prevent curling. Season both sides with salt and pepper.

2 Coat each cutlet lightly with flour, dip into beaten egg, and finally coat both sides with breadcrumbs.

3 Fill a heavy bottomed saucepan with oil to a depth of 3in, and heat to 350°F (180°C). Deep fry the cutlets one at a time for 5–7 minutes, turning once or twice until the meat is well cooked and golden brown.

4 Drain the cooked cutlets briefly on paper towels. Slice into 1in slices. Arrange each cutlet on a lettuce leaf so that it looks as though it is uncut. Garnish with lemon wedges and freshly made mustard.

5 Make *tonkatsu* sauce by combining Worcestershire sauce with ketchup, soy sauce, *sake* and mustard, adjusting the quantities to taste. Serve in small bowls as a dip.

DEEP-FRIED SOLE
(*Karei no kara age*)

Sole and other flatfish in season—and also trout, chicken and *tofu*—are delicious simply dusted with flour, cornstarch or *kuzu*, which forms a thin crisp film when the food is deep-fried.

INGREDIENTS (Serves 4)
4 3oz fillets of sole
salt
vegetable oil for deep frying
3 Tbsp kuzu or cornstarch
4 Tbsp grated daikon radish
2 Tbsp freshly grated ginger root
ponzu sauce (see page 77)

1. Lay the fish fillets on a cutting surface, dark side uppermost. With a sharp knife, make a shallow cross, about ¼in deep, in the top of each fillet. Sprinkle with a little salt and set aside to drain for at least one hour. Prepare the condiments while the fish is draining. Rinse in cold water and pat dry.

2. Heat plenty of oil in a small heavy saucepan to 340°F (170°C). Coat both sides of each fillet evenly with *kuzu* or cornstarch. Set the fish aside for a few minutes so that the coating can set.

3. Deep-fry the fillets one at a time for 4–5 minutes. Remove and drain on paper towels.

4. Arrange each fillet on a small plate on a folded napkin, and serve the condiments and sauce separately. The condiments are combined into the sauce, and then the fish dipped into the sauce before eating.

DEEP-FRIED POTATO
(*Jagaimo su-age*)

Carefully cut vegetables are best deep-fried very simply, without any coating or batter, so that their shape and color are not hidden. In this recipe, thin slices of potato are cut to look like *gingko* leaves, although any attractive shape will do. Make sure that the potatoes are dry before deep-frying. The deep-fry temperature for this dish is quite low. Any firm vegetable such as eggplants, French beans and sweet potatoes can be deep-fried simply in this way.

INGREDIENTS (Serves 4)
4 medium potatoes
vegetable oil for deep frying

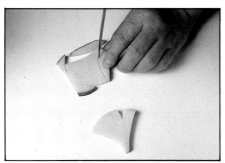

1 Slice the potatoes into ¼in thick slices. Cut each slice into a roughly triangular shape. Cut a notch in each triangle to make a *gingko* leaf.

2 Fill a heavy bottomed saucepan with oil to a depth of 2in, and heat to 315°F (160°C), or slightly higher. Put in a few potato slices and deep-fry quite slowly for 3–4 minutes, or until crisp and brown. Remove and drain on paper towels. Deep-fry the remaining slices a few at a time in the same way.

DEEP-FRIED PRAWN ROLLS
(*Ebi no isobe age*)

Prawns or shrimps rolled in *nori* seaweed and deep-fried have a lovely crisp texture and taste of the sea.

INGREDIENTS (Serves 4)
12 large prawns or jumbo shrimps
salt
12 sheets nori *seaweed, 2x1½in*
a little egg white
vegetable oil for deep frying

1 Peel the prawns or shrimps, leaving just the tails attached. To devein, insert a toothpick under the vein in the center of the back and pull up gently. Make three short cuts across the belly to prevent curling when the prawns are cooked. Rinse the prawns, pat dry and salt lightly.

2 Lay each prawn along the long side of a *nori* sheet. Roll up firmly.

3 Brush the edge with a little egg white and press to seal.

4 Heat plenty of oil in a small, heavy-bottomed saucepan to 340°F (170°C), and deep-fry the prawn rolls for 1–2 minutes. Drain briefly and serve hot.

ABOVE *Deep-fried foods are usually served on a neatly folded paper napkin. Deep-fried sole (top), potato (bottom left) and prawn rolls (bottom right) make an attractive dish garnished with a chrysanthemum leaf. Dipping sauce and condiments are served separately (top left).*

TEMPURA

The classic Japanese deep-fried dish is, of course, *tempura*: miraculously light morsels of fish and vegetables clad in a lacy golden batter. As in all Japanese cooking, the secret lies in lightness of touch. The batter, made with chilled ingredients, should be barely mixed, and rather lumpy, and should be made just before it is used. Ideally, *tempura* should be served straight from the pan, and in *tempura* restaurants in Japan it is cooked before the customers eyes and served up as it is cooked.

INGREDIENTS (Serves 4)
8 large prawns or jumbo shrimp, shelled and
   deveined, tails attached
2 medium onions
1 green pepper
1 medium carrot
4 oz mushrooms, wiped and trimmed,
   stems removed
1 eggplant
1 sheet (7x7in) nori seaweed
½ cup rice vermicelli (harusame) (optional)
4 sea scallops, washed and patted dry

DIPPING SAUCE
1¼ cups Dashi II
3 Tbsp light soy sauce
2 Tbsp mirin

BATTER
2 egg yolks
1 cup ice water
1 cup sifted flour
extra flour for dusting ingredients

CONDIMENTS
6 Tbsp (4in) grated daikon radish
2 Tbsp grated ginger

vegetable oil for deep frying

1 Score the belly of the prawns to prevent curling. Peel and halve the onions and cut across into slices, piercing with toothpicks to hold the rounds together. Core and deseed the pepper; halve and cut into strips. Cut the carrot into twists (*see* "Cutting techniques", page 42). Score a neat cross in the top of each mushroom. Cut the eggplant into fans (*see* "Cutting techniques"). With scissors, cut the *nori* seaweed in half. Cut one half into wide strips and set aside. Cut the other half into narrow strips and use to tie the rice vermicelli into bunches. Arrange all the ingredients, together with the batter ingredients, conveniently on a tray.

2 Combine the dipping sauce ingredients in a small saucepan, bring to a boil, and keep warm. Prepare the condiments.

3 Fill a small saucepan with oil to a depth of 3¼in, and heat to 325°F (170°C). While the oil is heating, prepare the batter. Place the egg yolks in a mixing bowl, add the ice water, and mix very lightly. Do not beat.

4 Add the flour all at once. Mix very lightly with chopsticks. The batter will be very lumpy.

5 Make sure that all the ingredients are perfectly dry. Dip the item of food to be fried in flour, and shake to remove excess.

6 Dip the food in the batter and place in the hot oil. Deep-fry for about 3 minutes until golden. Continue until all the ingredients are cooked, frying only a few items at a time.

7 Drain the cooked pieces of *tempura* on a rack or on paper towels for a few minutes. Arrange attractively on a neatly folded paper napkin and serve with warm dipping sauce and the condiments. The diners mix the condiments into the dipping sauce, and dip the *tempura* pieces into it before eating.

MIXED VEGETABLE TEMPURA (*Kaki age*)

A *tempura* meal often ends with a small portion of mixed vegetable *tempura*. Finely chopped vegetables are mixed into the remaining *tempura* batter and deep-fried to make delicate fritters.

INGREDIENTS (Serves 4)
2 medium carrots
1 onion
4oz French beans
batter as for tempura (see page 116)
vegetable oil for deep frying
dipping sauce and condiments as for tempura

1 Peel the carrots and cut into 2in julienne strips. Halve the onion and cut into thin slices. Top and tail the beans and cut into 2in lengths.

2 Lightly mix the vegetables with the batter

3 Heat the oil to 325°F (170°C). Slide the vegetable mixture by spoonfuls into the hot oil and deep-fry for about 1 minute on each side, until golden. Remove and drain on paper towels. Serve with warm dipping sauce and condiments.

ABOVE *Tempura (top) and mixed vegetable tempura (bottom) appetizingly arranged on paper napkins on bamboo trays. The dipping sauce (middle) is served separately.*

DEEP-FRIED SHRIMPS IN THICKENED BROTH
(*Ebi no ni oroshi*)

In this dish, deep-fried shrimps are served in—instead of with—a sauce, which is thickened with tangy *daikon* radish.

INGREDIENTS (Serves 4)
14oz shrimps
cornstarch or potato starch
vegetable oil for deep frying
1 cup grated <u>daikon</u> radish
1 cup <u>Dashi II</u>
4 Tbsp <u>mirin</u>
4 Tbsp light soy sauce
1 dried red chili pepper, seeded and very finely sliced
¼ cup fresh peas

1 Peel the shrimps, leaving just the tails attached. To devein, insert a toothpick under the vein in the center of the back and pull up gently. Rinse the shrimps and pat dry.

2 Sprinkle cornstarch or potato starch over the shrimps.

3 Preheat plenty of oil to 325°F (170°C). Carefully lower the shrimps into the oil by spoonfuls and deep-fry for 2–3 minutes, until golden. Remove and drain on paper towels.

4 Place the grated radish in a strainer and rinse in cold water. Squeeze the radish firmly and shape into a ball.

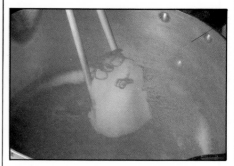

5 In a small saucepan, bring the *dashi* to a simmer. Add the *mirin*, soy sauce and the ball of grated radish, with sliced chili pepper on top.

6 Parboil the peas and add together with the shrimps. Bring back to a simmer and serve immediately in individual bowls.

DEEP-FRIED TOFU IN BROTH
(Agedashi-dofu)

Japan has a venerable tradition of vegetarianism and has developed delicious vegetarian dishes, many based on the protein-rich soybean. *Tofu* — soybean curd — is a favorite among younger Japanese as well as a staple for the older generation. In this dish, *tofu* is simply deep-fried, to make the most of its subtle flavor.

INGREDIENTS (Serves 4)
11oz tofu
2 Tbsp kuzu, *potato flour or cornstarch*

DIPPING SAUCE
1 cup Dashi II
3 Tbsp light soy sauce
3 Tbsp mirin

GARNISHES
⅓ cup daikon *radish*
1 Tbsp fresh ginger
1 scallion or young leek
1 Tbsp dried bonito flakes

vegetable oil for deep frying

1 First drain the *tofu:* set a weight such as a chopping board or dinner plate on the *tofu*. Set aside for at least 30 minutes to drain.

2 Grind the *kuzu* or flour finely in a *suribachi* or mortar and pestle; or simply crush with a rolling pin to make a fine powder.

3 Cut the drained *tofu* into four pieces and roll in the *kuzu* flour. Set aside.

4 Make the dipping sauces by combining the ingredients in a small saucepan, bring just to a simmer and keep warm.

5 Peel and grate the ginger. Set aside. Peel and grate the *daikon* radish and set aside.

6 Slice the scallion or leek into very fine slices. Place the bonito flakes in a small bowl.

7 Fill a small saucepan or deep-fryer with vegetable oil to a depth of 3in, and heat to 350°C (180°C).

8 Deep fry each piece of *tofu* separately for 6–8 minutes, until golden.

9 Drain the *tofu* briefly on paper towels. Arrange each piece of *tofu* on a serving dish, and top with the garnishes. Either pour the warm dipping sauce over or serve separately.

STEAMED DISHES
Mushimono

Steamed dishes provide an opportunity to create the most beautiful pictures with food. The various ingredients are artistically arranged in the dishes in which they will be served before being lightly steamed, a process which conserves the natural flavor and goodness of the food, keeping it moist and tender, as well as heightening the color. It is a technique particularly appropriate to Japanese cuisine. Vegetables, fish and seafood are often steamed, and steamed chicken is a particular favorite. Most food is steamed without seasoning and served with a thickened and seasoned sauce, or occasionally with a rich topping.

The Japanese use flat steamers which can be stacked like Chinese bamboo steamers—a folding steamer cannot be used for Japanese steamed dishes. A steamer can be improvised by using a large saucepan, in which is set a rack to support the dish above the level of the water. It is best to lay a cloth over the top of the pan, under the lid, to absorb excess moisture.

Foods should always be put into a hot steamer already full of steam. Most foods are steamed over high heat and, as always in Japanese cooking, for as short a time as possible.

SAKE-STEAMED CHICKEN
(Tori no saka mushi)

Fresh chicken, lightly steamed, is a great favorite in Japan. It needs only a little seasoning, and is served with a couple of piquant dipping sauces.

INGREDIENTS (Serves 4)
11oz boned chicken breast, skin attached
1 Tbsp salt
2 Tbsp sake
½ cucumber
4 leaves lettuce
4 lemon wedges
freshly made wasabi
3 Tbsp dark soy sauce
ponzu sauce (see page 77)
red maple radish (see page 77)
1 young leek, shredded and rinsed (see "Cutting techniques", page 41)

1 Put the chicken in a bowl, skin-side up, and score the skin with a fork. Sprinkle with salt and *sake* and set aside for 20 minutes to marinate.

2 Steam the chicken, uncovered, in a preheated steamer over high heat for 15 to 20 minutes, until just cooked. allow to cool and slice into ¾in pieces.

3 Cut the cucumber into 2in lengths, and cut lengthways into paper-thin slices. Salt lightly, knead, rinse and pat dry.

4 Wash the lettuce leaves and pat dry. Lay them on four small plates. Arrange the chicken slices on the lettuce leaves, and garnish with cucumber slices and lemon wedges.

5 Prepare the *wasabi* and serve with soy sauce. Serve the *ponzu* sauce with red maple radish and shredded leek.

SAKE-STEAMED SOLE
(Karei no sake mushi)

Sake-steaming is a delicious way of bringing out the subtle flavor of any flat fish. The result is often served with piquant *ponzu* sauce and grated *daikon* radish or simple maple radish.

INGREDIENTS (Serves 4)
4 3oz fillets of sole
salt
1 piece <u>kombu</u> seaweed, about 3x3in
1 cup <u>sake</u>

DIPPING SAUCE
1 cup <u>ponzu</u> sauce (see page 77)
1 cup light soy sauce
¼ cup <u>mirin</u>
½ cup <u>Dashi II</u>

CONDIMENTS
1 young leek, shredded and rinsed
(see "Cutting techniques" page 41)
red maple radish (see page 77)

1 Lay the fillets on a cutting surface with the dark side uppermost. With a sharp knife make a shallow cross about ¼in deep in the top of each fillet. Sprinkle the fillets with a little salt and set aside to drain for at least 1 hour. Rinse in cold water and pat dry.

2 Prepare four deep plates for steaming. Wipe the *kombu* and place one piece in each plate. On each, put one fillet scored side up. Pour *sake* generously over the fillets and *kombu*. Cover with plastic wrap or foil, sealing the edges tightly. Place in a preheated steamer and steam for 15 minutes.

3 While the fish is steaming, prepare the dipping sauce. Combine the dipping sauce ingredients in a small saucepan and bring to a simmer; pour into four small bowls. Arrange small mounds of the condiments on individual plates. Serve the fish piping hot with the dipping sauce and condiments.

SAKE-STEAMED CLAMS
(Hamaguri no saka mushi)

Clams are a food for special occasions and, served in their shells, make an elegant dish. *Sake* is used to accentuate the flavor.

INGREDIENTS (Serves 4)
8 large hard-shelled clams
4 pieces <u>kombu</u> seaweed, about 3x3in
½ cup <u>sake</u>
½ tsp salt
1 bunch watercress, divided into 4
4 thin slices lemon

1 Put the clams in lightly salted water to cover. Leave in a dark cool place for 24 hours, to allow the clams to expel sand.

2 Rinse the clams thoroughly, wipe the *kombu,* and place in four deep plates for steaming. Sprinkle sake over the clams and *kombu* and season lightly with salt.

3 Cover with plastic wrap or foil, sealing the edges tightly, and place in a preheated steamer. Steam for 10 minutes, until the clams open.

4 Remove the wrap or foil, add the watercress, and steam uncovered for a few seconds. Serve with a slice of lemon.

SALMON STEAMED WITH ROE
(Sake no oyako mushi)

The best salmon is found in colder climates. In Japan, the salmon from Tohoku in the north of the main island of Honshu is said to be the most delicious. This dish, using both the salmon and its roe, is named, rather touchingly *"oyako"*, "parent and child".

INGREDIENTS (Serves 4)
12oz salmon fillets, boned and skinned
salt
vegetable oil
¼ cup salmon roe
2 Tbsp sake
½ cup grated daikon radish, drained
1 egg

SAUCE
1 cup Dashi II
3 Tbsp mirin
2 Tbsp rice vinegar
2 Tbsp light soy sauce
2 tsp cornstarch mixed with 2 tsp
  water
1 lemon
1 young leek, shredded and rinsed (see
  "Cutting techniques", page 41)

1 Salt the salmon, (*see* "Salting fish", page 37) and slice it thinly.

2 Place in a lightly oiled frying pan and fry for 1–2 minutes on each side to seal the flavor.

3 Immediately remove to a strainer and rinse with cold water.

4 Mix the roe with the *sake* in a small bowl to clean the roe; strain and discard the liquid.

5 Mix the radish with the egg and season with a little salt. Stir the roe into the radish and egg mixture.

6 Divide the salmon pieces evenly among four small bowls, and spoon the roe mixture over the salmon.

7 Cover with plastic wrap or foil, sealing the edges tightly. Place in a preheated steamer; steam for 5 minutes over high heat.

8 While the salmon is steaming, prepare the sauce. In a small saucepan, bring the *dashi, mirin,* vinegar and soy sauce to a simmer. Turn the heat to low, add the cornstarch solution, and stir continuously until the sauce thickens.

9 Remove the bowls from the steamer, uncover, and spoon the thickened sauce over the salmon pieces.

10 Squeeze a little lemon onto each portion, top with a few shreds of leek and serve.

SHINSHU-STYLE STEAMED SEA TROUT
(*Suzuki no shinshu mushi*)

The mountainous Shinshu area of northern Honshu is famous for its buckwheat noodles (*Soba*).

INGREDIENTS (Serves 4)
1 sea trout, about 18oz
salt
4 dried mushrooms, reconstituted (see page 39)
1 young leek, shredded and rinsed (see page 41)
4oz dried buckwheat noodles
4 2in pieces kombu seaweed, wiped
sake

SAUCE
3 ¾ cups Dashi II
1 cup dark soy sauce
½ cup mirin

freshly made wasabi (see page 76)

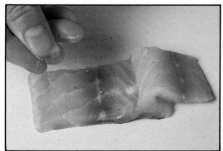

1 Fillet the fish using the three-piece filleting technique (*see* page 35). Cut the fish into four slices; or use four ready-cut fillets. Slice each fillet and open it out like a book. Lightly salt both sides and set aside for 40 minutes to one hour. Simmer the mushrooms in their soaking water for 20 minutes until tender, and prepare the leek.

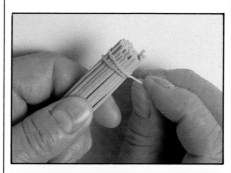

2 Separate the noodles into four bunches, and tie each bunch securely at the base. Put into plenty of rapidly boiling salted water. Boil for 10 minutes until the noodles are tender; do not add cold water.

3 Remove the noodles and immediately place in cold water.

4 Rinse the fish slices and pat dry. Lay the free end of the noodles over the open fish slice, and fold over the fish to enclose the noodles like a sandwich.

5 Fold the tied end of the noodles over the fish, then cut away the tied end. Repeat with the remaining slices of fish.

6 Divide the *kombu* pieces among four ovenproof bowls, and carefully place the fish and noodles on the *kombu*. Place a drained mushroom in each bowl. Sprinkle a little *sake* over each piece of fish. Cover the bowls tightly with plastic wrap or foil, and steam in a preheated steamer for 10 minutes.

7 Combine the *dashi*, soy sauce and *mirin* in a small saucepan and bring to a boil. Remove the fish from the steamer and ladle the hot sauce over the fillets. Garnish with shredded leek and a little *wasabi*, and serve immediately.

SAVORY STEAMED CUSTARD
(*Chawan Mushi*)

No Japanese kitchen would be complete without a set of lidded *chawan mushi* cups, for *chawan mushi*—a delicate steamed custard in which float morsels of chicken, fish and vegetables—is a classic Japanese dish. Although less aesthetically pleasing, it may be made in ordinary mugs or ramekins, tightly-lidded with foil. *Chawan mushi* is one of the very few Japanese dishes which is eaten with a spoon instead of chopsticks.

INGREDIENTS (Serves 4)
3oz boned chicken breast
1 tsp sake
1 Tbsp light soy sauce
4 shrimps, shelled and deveined
  salt
4 large mushrooms, wiped, stems removed

CUSTARD
4 eggs
2 ½ cups Dashi I
½ tsp salt
1 Tbsp mirin

1 bunch watercress

1 Cut the chicken into ½in cubes, sprinkle with *sake* and soy sauce, and set aside for a few minutes to marinate. Sprinkle the shrimps with a little salt. Halve the mushroom caps.

2 Mix the eggs lightly in a small bowl so that the mixture does not become frothy. Stir in the *dashi*, salt and *mirin*.

3 Divide the chicken pieces, shrimps and mushrooms among four cups.

4 Pour the egg mixture over the ingredients in the cups. Cover each cup with a lid or foil and steam in a preheated steamer over medium heat for 15 minutes, until the custard is just set; it will still be very soft. Add a little watercress to each cup just before steaming finishes. Serve very hot.

VINEGARED SALADS
Sunomono

At the start of a restaurant meal, you will be served tiny portions of different salads as an hors d'oeuvre. A salad may also be served at the end of the meal, just before the rice. Most family meals include a cold dish made up of ingredients selected for their color as well as their taste, heaped in dainty mounds in small deep bowls of contrasting color and shape.

A Japanese salad is rather different from a Western one. Traditionally vegetables were never eaten raw, and even today vegetables are usually salted or parboiled before being included in salad. Seaweeds and seafoods are also very common ingredients.

Like all cooks, Japanese chefs enjoy experimenting with exotic fruits and vegetables, which have only recently become available in Japan, to make spectacular combinations. There is a great variety of salad dressings, all of which are oil-free. Salad ingredients should always be cool or chilled and perfectly dry.

A vinegared salad may consist simply of one or two vegetables, finely shredded, or a rich mixture of fruit and vegetables with fish, shellfish or meat. The dressing will probably be a piquant combination of rice vinegar and *dashi*, subtly flavored with soy sauce and a little sugar—or a hint of ginger, *wasabi*, sesame or lemon.

BEEF SALAD IN HOT CHILI DRESSING
(*Gyuniku no namban ae*)

In the sixteenth century, the few Westerners who managed to make their way to Japan were known as *"namban"*— barbarians from the south. They brought with them red peppers, which also became known as *"namban"*, as well as the outlandish habit of eating meat. The name of this salad could equally be translated "Beef salad southern barbarian style". You may substitute 4-5 okra, parboiled, for the Japanese yam.

INGREDIENTS (Serves 4)
½–¾ cup Japanese yam (or 4-5 okra, parboiled)
½ cucumber
1 young leek or scallion
1 1in piece ginger root
10oz fillet of beef
salt and pepper
vegetable oil for frying

DRESSING
2 pickled plums (umeboshi)
1 Tbsp miso
3 Tbsp rice vinegar
1 red chili pepper, seeded and very finely sliced
1 Tbsp sugar
1 tsp sesame oil

4 sprigs watercress to garnish

1 Wash the vegetables and pat dry. Cut the yam and cucumber into "poem cards" (*see* "Cutting techniques", page 40). Lightly salt and set aside to drain. Sliver the leek or scallion and cut the ginger into threads (*see* "needle cut", page 41).

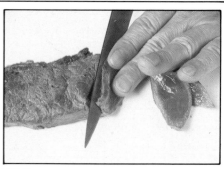

2 Lightly brush a frying pan with oil and fry the beef until both sides are lightly browned. Slice the beef very finely and season with salt and pepper.

3 Seed the pickled plums. Mash the plum flesh with the *miso* in a *suribachi*.

4 Combine the vinegar, ½ the chili pepper and the sugar in a small saucepan and heat to dissolve the sugar. Remove from heat and cool. Blend the cooled vinegar mixture with the pickled plum and *miso*, and finally stir in the sesame oil.

5 | Rub the mixture through a sieve to purée. Rinse the yam and cucumber and pat dry. Arrange the beef and vegetables in four small deep bowls and pour the dressing over them. Garnish each dish with a sprig of watercress and a few slices of red chili pepper.

MIXED SALAD PLATE
(*Yuzen ae*)

This dish relies for its appeal on the qualities of the ingredients themselves, which are prepared very simply with only the lightest of seasoning, and arranged individually to make a colorful display. Characteristic of much of Japanese cooking, the plain tastes of the ingredients are complimented by a piquant dipping sauce. The combination of ingredients, ranging from the exotic kiwi fruit to chicken and fine noodles, is actually quite bold. Use your imagination to create your own combinations.

INGREDIENTS (Serves 4)
4oz boned white chicken meat
pinch of salt
1 Tbsp sake
2oz harusame *noodles*
¼ cup omelet strips (see page 98)
½ cucumber
4 leaves red cabbage
1 medium carrot
8 leaves lettuce
1 bunch watercress
1 lemon
½ Tbsp wakame *seaweed, reconstituted*
    (see "Preparing dried foods", page 39)
1 kiwi fruit

DRESSING
*3 pickled plums (*umeboshi*)*
3 Tbsp Dashi II
3 Tbsp mirin
4 Tbsp rice vinegar
1 tsp salt
2 tsp sugar
1 tsp kuzu, *potato flour or cornstarch*

1 Season the chicken with salt and *sake*. Place in a bowl and steam in a preheated steamer over high heat for 20 minutes. Allow to cool. Shred the chicken.

2 Drop the *harusame* noodles into rapidly boiling salted water and boil for 4-5 minutes until soft. Rinse in cold water several times and set aside to drain.

3 Prepare the omelet strips (*see* page 98).

4 Cut the cucumber into "poem cards" (*see* page 40). Slice the cabbage and carrot into threads (*see* page 41). Place in cold water.

5 Wash the lettuce and watercress and pat dry. Slice the lemon. With a sharp knife, cut the *wakame* seaweed into 1in lengths. Peel and slice the kiwi fruit.

6 Seed the pickled plums and rub the plum flesh through a sieve. Stir in the other dressing ingredients. Cook the mixture over a very low heat, stirring frequently, until it thickens.

7 Drain the cucumber, cabbage and carrot and pat dry. Arrange all the ingredients on an attractive tray or platter. Serve the dressing separately as a dipping sauce.

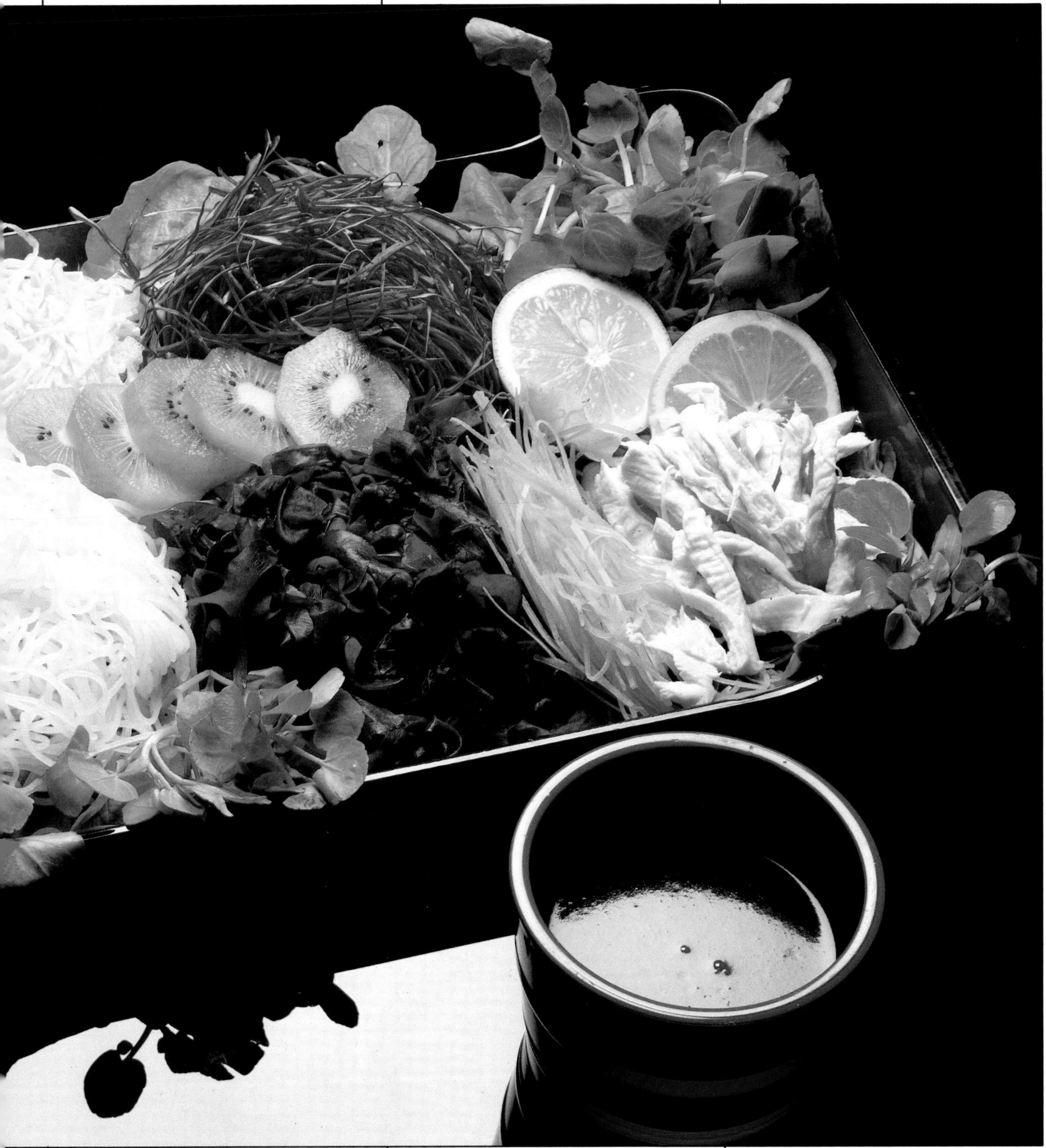

CRAB AND CUCUMBER SALAD (*Kanisu*)

This simple, elegant salad combines cucumber and crab. Fresh crab is a favorite in Japan. Boil or steam and remove the crab meat in large chunks.

INGREDIENTS (Serves 4)
½ cucumber
½ tsp salt
8 lettuce heart leaves
¾ cup crab meat
2 Tbsp freshly grated ginger root

1 Cut the cucumber into 2in lengths and slice thinly to make "poem cards" (*see* "Cutting techniques", page 40).

2 Dissolve ½ tsp salt in ½ cup cold water. Add the cucumber and leave to soak for 20 minutes. Squeeze gently to remove excess moisture, and pat dry with paper towels.

3 Prepare four glass goblets or attractive salad bowls and arrange two lettuce leaves in each. Arrange the crab meat and cucumber slices on the lettuce.

4 With your fingers, squeeze ginger juice from the grated ginger over each dish and serve.

CRAB AND CUCUMBER ROLLS (*Kanisu*)

With typical Japanese flair, the shape and muted color of the crab and cucumber are used to produce a visually-appealing dish. A bamboo rolling mat is very helpful in making good firm rolls.

INGREDIENTS (Serves 4)
½ cucumber
½ tsp salt
*2 large or 4 small rectangular egg
  sheets (omelets)*
¾ cup crab meat
3 Tbsp rice vinegar
2 Tbsp freshly grated ginger root

1 Cut the cucumber into 2in lengths and slice thinly to make "poem cards" (*see* "Cutting techniques", page 40).

2 Dissolve ½ tsp salt in ½ cup cold water, add the cucumber and leave to soak for 20 minutes. Squeeze gently to remove excess moisture and pat dry with paper towels.

3 Arrange all the ingredients in preparation for the roll. Lay one egg sheet on a bamboo rolling mat. Arrange a wide band of crab meat along the near end; lay a line of cucumber slices along the crab meat.

4 Holding the crab meat and cucumber firmly in place with your fingers, roll the bamboo mat over with your thumbs to enclose them, making sure that they remain in the center of the roll (this may be a little tricky the first time). Gently press the mat around the roll to shape it.

5 Leaving the mat behind, continue to roll up the egg sheet until the roll is nearly complete.

6 Brush a little vinegar along the edge of the roll and finish rolling, pressing gently to seal. Leave the roll to rest for a few minutes with the sealed edge underneath. Repeat with the remaining ingredients to make another large roll or three small rolls.

7 Wet a very sharp knife and cut each roll into slices 1-2in long, wetting the knife several times as you cut. Arrange two or three slices in individual dishes and serve.

ABOVE *Crab and cucumber rolls (left) and crab and cucumber salad (right) make elegant and refreshing summer dishes.*

137

RED AND WHITE SALAD
(*Kohaku namasu*)

Red and white are auspicious colors in Japan. This salad of red carrot and white *daikon* radish is served on festive occasions.

INGREDIENTS (Serves 4)
4in daikon radish
1 medium carrot
½ tsp salt

DRESSING
3 Tbsp rice vinegar
3 Tbsp mirin
1 Tbsp Dashi II
pinch salt

1 piece 1½in sq kombu seaweed
shredded orange or lemon rind to garnish

1 Scrape the *daikon* radish and carrot. Cut into "needles" (*see* "Vegetable cutting", page 41)

2 Salt the vegetables and set aside for 10 minutes. Knead thoroughly until the *daikon* radish becomes soft and translucent, then squeeze to press out as much water as possible

3 Combine the dressing ingredients in a small saucepan and bring to a boil. Remove from heat and chill. Add 2 Tbsp of the chilled dressing to the vegetables. Mix and knead; squeeze to press out the dressing. Discard the excess dressing.

4 Put the *kombu* in a clean bowl and put the vegetables on top. Pour the remaining dressing over them. Cover the bowl and refrigerate for at least 30 minutes—the salad will have a better flavor if it is left overnight. Refrigerated in a tightly sealed container, it will keep for up to 2 weeks.

5 Serve cold or at room temperature in small portions, garnished with a few shreds of orange or lemon peel.

CUCUMBER AND WAKAME SALAD
(*Kyuri to wakame no sunomono*)

Silky fronds of *wakame* seaweed and cucumber, in a light vinegar dressing, makes a refreshing dish which is a classic of Japanese home cooking.

INGREDIENTS *(Serves 4)*
1 cucumber or 2 small Japanese cucumbers
½ tsp salt
1 Tbsp dried <u>wakame</u> seaweed, reconstituted (see "Preparing dried foods", page 39)

DRESSING
3 Tbsp rice vinegar
2 Tbsp <u>Dashi II</u>
2 Tbsp soy sauce
1 Tbsp sugar
¼ tsp salt
2 Tbsp <u>mirin</u>

GARNISH
1 Tbsp ginger, chopped into fine needles (see "Cutting techniques", page 41)

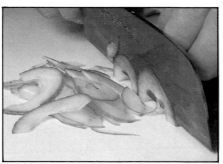

1 Slice the cucumber in half lengthways. Scrape out the seeds. Cut into paper-thin slices.

2 Dissolve ½ tsp salt in ½ cup cold water, add the cucumber, and leave to soak for 20 minutes. Put the cucumber into cheesecloth to drain.

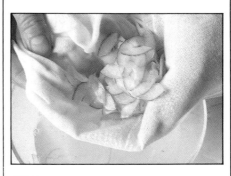

3 Squeeze the cucumber gently to remove excess moisture.

4 Combine the dressing ingredients in a small saucepan, and heat to dissolve the sugar. Remove from heat and chill. Trim the *wakame* seaweed and chop coarsely. Combine the *wakame* and cucumber in a bowl and spoon the chilled dressing over them. Toss gently.

5 Arrange neat mounds of salad in individual bowls. Garnish with a little chopped ginger.

ABOVE *Red and white salad (left), and cucumber and <u>wakame</u> salad (right). Small mounds of salad are heaped in the center of attractive porcelain bowls.*

DRESSED SALADS
Aemono

Tofu, flavored with sesame, a dash of sugar and salt—and sometimes with *miso* or vinegar—provides the basis for many of the thick creamy dressings which are served with vegetables, meat, fish, seafood and seaweeds in varying combinations. Dressed salads are richer and more substantial than the more piquant vinegared salads. The high protein content of *tofu* makes them very nutritious.

Tofu needs to be lightly drained for use in salads; it can be wrapped in clean towels and left for 30 minutes, or placed under a weight, such as a chopping board. Once drained, it readily absorbs flavors, making it a very versatile food.

Dressing may also be based on sesame seeds or peanuts, on *miso* or on any number of other ingredients.

FRENCH BEANS WITH PEANUT DRESSING
(*Ingen no peanut ae*)

French beans, lightly cooked so that they are still crunchy, are mixed with a tasty peanut dressing to make a simple and popular salad. If you do not have a *suribachi*, grind the peanuts in an electric grinder before adding the remaining dressing ingredients.

INGREDIENTS (Serves 4)
6oz French beans
salt

DRESSING
1/4 cup peanuts, roasted
1 1/2 Tbsp sugar
2 Tbsp soy sauce
1-2 Tbsp <u>Dashi II</u>, if required (see recipe, page 58)

1/2 tsp dried bonito flakes

1 Wash and trim the beans. Parboil in lightly salted boiling water until just tender. Drain and refresh in cold water. Slice diagonally into 1 1/2in lengths. Pat dry.

2 Place the peanuts in a *suribachi* and grind finely.

3 Blend in the remaining dressing ingredients, adding enough *dashi* to make a thick paste.

4 Add the beans and stir well to coat with dressing. Arrange small portions of the salad in deep individual bowls and garnish with bonito flakes.

WHITE SALAD
(*Shiro ae*)

Finely chopped vegetables, combined with a creamy *tofu* and sesame dressing, is the classic dressed salad. There are as many variations, both in the ingredients and in the dressing, as there are homes in Japan. Vegetables are never used raw, but may be salted or parboiled, or simmered in a rich stock to develop a strong flavor and thus complement the dressing. Vegetables and dressing may be prepared beforehand, but should be combined only at the last minute.

INGREDIENTS (Serves 4)
3 dried mushrooms, reconstituted (see
  "Preparing dried foods", page 39)
2 tsp soy sauce
1 tsp mirin
1 cup daikon radish
1 small carrot
salt
½ cake (4oz) konnyaku (arrum root jelly)
  (optional)
2oz French beans

DRESSING
7oz tofu
1 Tbsp white sesame seeds
2½ Tbsp white miso
1 Tbsp mirin
1 tsp sugar

1 sheet nori seaweed

1 Remove the stems of the mushrooms and slice thinly. Place in a small saucepan and add the soy sauce and *mirin;* simmer over very low heat for 10-15 minutes. Leave the mushrooms in any remaining stock to cool.

2 Cut the *daikon* radish and carrot into threads (*see* "Cutting techniques", page 41). Salt and set aside for 10 minutes, then knead until the vegetables become soft. Rinse, squeeze out excess moisture and pat dry.

3 Rub the *konnyaku* with salt, then rinse and pound with a rolling pin or a wooden pestle. Cut into julienne strips. Sauté in a dry frying pan for a few minutes, then set aside to cool. Top and tail the beans and parboil.

4 Wrap the *tofu* in clean dry towels, weight with a chopping board and set aside for 20-30 minutes to drain. Press the *tofu* through a sieve.

5 Toast the sesame seeds with a little salt in a dry frying pan. When they give off a nutty aroma, transfer to a *suribachi* and grind until oily. Blend in the *tofu* and the remaining dressing ingredients.

6 Make sure the vegetables are all perfectly dry, and stir into the dressing. Mound the salad in small deep individual bowls. Lightly toast the *nori* seaweed and cut with scissors into threads. Set a small mound of *nori* on each serving to garnish.

CLAMS IN THEIR SHELLS WITH SPICY MISO
(*Hamaguri to wakegi no karashi sumiso*)

Shellfish—accompanied by the youngest, freshest leeks available—makes a delicious salad. The preparation of this dish is simple, relying on the quality of the ingredients. The finished dish is most sophisticated. *Miso* with the tang of hot mustard complements the flavor of clams particularly well; serve only a small amount of the strongly flavored *miso* with each portion.

INGREDIENTS *(Serves 4)*
4 large hard-shelled clams
4 fresh young leeks, washed and trimmed
salt

DRESSING
½ cup sweet <u>miso</u> (see grilled eggplant, page 108)
1 Tbsp rice vinegar
½ tsp powdered mustard, mixed to a paste with a little water
3 Tbsp <u>Dashi II</u>

lightly toasted sesame seeds to garnish

2 Cut the leeks into 2in chunks and parboil in lightly salted boiling water; drain and set aside to cool. Pat dry.

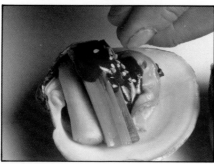

3 Blend the dressing ingredients (preferably in a *suribachi*), adding sufficient *dashi* to give the consistency of mayonnaise. Arrange the clams and leeks in the shells and spoon the *miso* over them. Garnish with a few toasted sesame seeds.

1 Put the clams in lightly salted water to cover. Leave in a dark place for 4-5 hours. Wash thoroughly and put in a saucepan with cold water to cover. Bring to a boil, adding 1 tsp salt just before the water boils. Simmer for 2-3 minutes, until the clams open. Drain. When cool enough to handle, cut the clams from their shells with a sharp knife, and cut each into 3 pieces. Wash the shells, scraping the insides.

ONE-POT COOKERY
Nabemono

One-pot cookery is a great winter favorite in Japan. The whole family gathers at the table, on which is a pot of simmering broth. Carefully arranged on a platter nearby are vegetables; meat, fish and *tofu,* all neatly chopped ready to cook. Everyone shares in the cooking, filling the pot with the raw ingredients and helping themselves to a portion of meat and vegetables when they are just to their taste. The piping hot morsels of food are dipped into a small bowl of sauce seasoned with some of the condiments which are spread around the table. This convivial activity usually takes up the whole evening.

A few pieces of equipment are practically essential for one-pot cookery. You will need a small gas or electric burner which can be used on the table, and a large and attractive lidded ovenproof casserole—in Japan, earthenware or cast iron casseroles are used (*see* "Utensils"). You will also need chopsticks for putting food into and taking it out of the casserole, and a ladle for dishing out stock. If necessary, the food can be cooked in the kitchen and brought to the table piping hot; but although the taste may be the same, the atmosphere would be missing.

Practically any seasonal food can be used in one-pot cookery. Use twice as many vegetables as meat or fish. All the ingredients should be cut into quite small pieces that will cook quickly; hard vegetables are usually parboiled. A one-pot recipe is a meal in itself. It needs only to be followed with rice and pickles.

SUKIYAKI, TOKYO STYLE

Sukiyaki, perhaps Japan's most famous food, is a classic one-pot dish. Finest quality beef and vegetables are lightly cooked in a broth which, as the meal progresses, gradually becomes more and more rich and tasty with the juices of the cooking foods. Raw egg makes a surprisingly delicious dipping sauce. Japanese cooks buy their *sukiyaki* beef ready-sliced; ask your butcher to slice it into paper-thin slices on a bacon slicer. To slice it yourself, first put it in the freezer to stiffen it, and then slice it as thin as possible.

INGREDIENTS (Serves 4)
7oz tofu
12 flat mushrooms, wiped and trimmed
1 package (7oz) shirataki noodles
7oz napa cabbage
1 onion
4 leeks, washed and trimmed
18oz top sirloin beef, in paper-thin slices

SAUCE
1 cup Dashi II
1 cup soy sauce
1 cup mirin
1 Tbsp sugar

4 eggs
vegetable oil

1 Cut the *tofu* into 1½in squares. Remove the stems of the mushrooms and cut a cross in the top of each. Parboil the *shirataki* for 1-2 minutes and drain. Wash the cabbage, slice across into 1½in lengths, then quarter each segment. Pat dry. Peel the onion, halve and slice. Cut the leeks diagonally into 1½in lengths. Arrange the ingredients attractively on a large platter; do not mix the ingredients.

2 Combine the sauce ingredients and bring to a boil; transfer to a jug. Each diner breaks an egg into a bowl and beats it.

3 A large, deep skillet or an electric frying pan is best for *sukiyaki.* Heat the pan over medium heat and brush with oil. Add slices of beef in a single layer and brown both sides.

4 Add small quantities of all the other ingredients and pour over a little of the sauce. Continue to cook over a medium heat, replenishing the pot with meat, vegetables and sauce as required.

5 Before eating, dip the cooked meat and vegetables into raw egg.

ABOVE *Before the <u>sukiyaki</u> meal begins, all the ingredients are laid out on the table, making an appetizing display: (clockwise) prime beef, mushrooms, leeks, onions, napa cabbage, <u>shirataki</u> noodles, carrots, <u>tofu</u>; (around central platter) heavy cast iron <u>sukiyaki</u> pan on a portable gas burner, jug of sauce, china spoon for serving, rice, beaten egg for dipping, raw eggs, butter or oil.*

SHABU SHABU

A *shabu shabu* meal is always an occasion, as everyone dips paper-thin slices of the finest beef together with immaculately fresh vegetables into a delicate stock, gently moving them in the stock to make a sound which, to the Japanese ear, sounds like "shabu shabu". Tradition offers a choice of rich dipping sauces and condiments. Finally the stock itself, in which all the flavors of the cooking foods have accumulated, is served as a delicious soup.

INGREDIENTS (Serves 4)
7oz *tofu*
7oz napa cabbage
½ cup spinach, washed and trimmed
1 cup bamboo shoots
12 flat mushrooms, wiped and trimmed
1 package (7oz) *shirataki* *noodles*
4 leeks, washed and trimmed
18oz top sirloin of beef, in
*   paper-thin slices*

SESAME SAUCE
2 Tbsp white sesame seeds
salt
3 Tbsp *Dashi II*
2 Tbsp rice vinegar
2 Tbsp light soy sauce
1 Tbsp *mirin*

soy sauce
red maple radish (see page 77)
grated *daikon* *radish*
lemon wedges
shredded and rinsed scallions or leeks (see
*   "Cutting techniques", page 41)*
1 piece *kombu* *seaweed, 4in sq*

1 Cut the *tofu* into 1½in squares. Wash the cabbage and cut into large chunks; parboil in plenty of rapidly-boiling salted water for 2-3 minutes, then drain well and pat dry. Wash the bamboo shoots and cut into "poem cards" (*see* page 40)

2 Remove the stems of the mushrooms and cut a cross in the top of each. Parboil the *shirataki* for 1-2 minutes and drain. Cut the leeks diagonally into 1in lengths. Arrange the ingredients attractively on a large platter, grouping each type of ingredient together.

3 Lightly toast the sesame seeds with a little salt until golden brown. Transfer to a *suribachi* and grind until oily. Gradually blend in the remaining sesame sauce ingredients. Pour into small individual bowls for dipping. Fill four other small bowls with soy sauce and prepare and distribute the condiments in yet more bowls.

4 Wipe the *kombu* and make a few slashes in it to help release the flavor. Place in a large ovenproof casserole and fill three-quarters full of water. Bring to a boil and remove the *kombu*. It is now up to the diners to cook the meal. With chopsticks, pick up slices of beef and move them around in the simmering stock for ½ minute, until the meat becomes pink. Dip into one of the sauces and eat immediately.

5 Continue to cook the ingredients. Allow the vegetables to cook for a little longer than the meat. When all the ingredients have been consumed, ladle the broth into bowls, season with a little salt, and serve as soup.

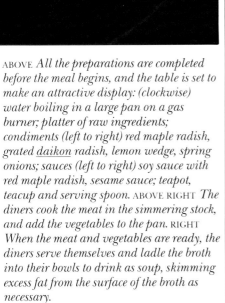

ABOVE *All the preparations are completed before the meal begins, and the table is set to make an attractive display: (clockwise) water boiling in a large pan on a gas burner; platter of raw ingredients; condiments (left to right) red maple radish, grated* daikon *radish, lemon wedge, spring onions; sauces (left to right) soy sauce with red maple radish, sesame sauce; teapot, teacup and serving spoon.* ABOVE RIGHT *The diners cook the meat in the simmering stock, and add the vegetables to the pan.* RIGHT *When the meat and vegetables are ready, the diners serve themselves and ladle the broth into their bowls to drink as soup, skimming excess fat from the surface of the broth as necessary.*

RIVERBANK OYSTER CASSEROLE
(*Kaki dote nabe*)

Japan's oysters are harvested from the Inland Sea and appear in the winter on tables throughout the land. Oysters and *miso* make a particularly delicious combination, and in this one-pot dish the whole casserole is coated with a thick layer of *miso* like the bank of a river. The layer is scraped little by little into the simmering broth.

INGREDIENTS (Serves 4)
6 large oysters, shucked
salt
4 scallions or young leeks
7oz napa cabbage
7oz tofu

MISO "RIVERBANK"
4 Tbsp red miso
1 cup white miso
5 Tbsp mirin

1 piece kombu seaweed, 4in sq
5 cups Dashi II
4 eggs

1 Gently wash the oysters in lightly salted water. Rinse separately under cold running water and drain. Wash and trim the vegetables. Cut the scallions or leeks into 2in lengths, separating the white and the green parts. Halve the napa cabbage lengthways and cut into 2in chunks. Cut the *tofu* into 1½in squares.

2 Mix together the two *misos* and the *mirin* to make a thick but spreadable paste—you may need to dilute the mixture with a little *dashi*. Spread the paste to coat the inside of an ovenproof casserole, making a thick bank all around the edge.

3 Wipe the *kombu* and make a few slashes in it; lay in the casserole. Arrange the oysters, vegetables and *tofu* attractively on the *kombu*.

4 Bring the casserole to table and set over a low flame. Heat for a few minutes to roast the *miso*. Add enough *dashi* to cover the ingredients and bring to a boil. Continue to simmer. The diners help themselves to the cooked ingredients directly from the casserole, dipping each ingredient into a small bowl of beaten raw egg. The oysters are ready when they swell and the edges curl; oysters become tough if they are overcooked.

CASSEROLE OF COD
(*Tara chiri nabe*)

Fish gives a rich flavor to the simmering stock, and is a popular ingredient for one-pot dishes. Ideally a whole fish, preferably straight from the ocean, is used. It is filleted (*see* "Cutting techniques", page 35) and cut into large chunks; the bones and head are used to enrich the stock. Fresh fillets or steaks are also suitable for this dish; do not use frozen fish. Any firm-fleshed white fish such as flounder, haddock, sea trout or sea bass may be used in place of the cod.

INGREDIENTS (Serves 4)
4 cod steaks, each 5oz
7oz napa cabbage
1 medium carrot
2 young leeks
8 large flat mushrooms, wiped and trimmed
7oz tofu
1 package (7oz) shirataki noodles
ponzu sauce (see page 77)
red maple radish (see page 77)
scallions or young leeks, shredded and rinsed (see "Cutting techniques", page 41)
lemon wedges
1 piece kombu seaweed, 4in sq

1 Cut the fish into 1½in chunks. Separate the napa cabbage leaves, cut into large chunks and parboil. Cut the carrots into florettes (*see* "Cutting techniques", page 43). Wash and trim the leeks and cut into 2in lengths. Remove the stems of the mushrooms and cut a cross in the top of each. Cut the *tofu* into bite size cubes. Parboil the *shirataki* for 1-2 minutes and drain. Arrange the ingredients attractively on a large platter. Prepare and distribute the sauce and condiments.

2 Wipe the *kombu* and make a few slashes in it. Fill an ovenproof casserole three-quarters full with water, add the *kombu,* and bring to a boil, removing the *kombu* just before the water boils.

3 The diners now add a little of each ingredient to the pot, adding some fish first to flavor the stock, and helping themselves from the pot when the ingredients are just tender. The condiments are mixed into the *ponzu* sauce, which is used as a dipping sauce.

MIXED WINTER CASSEROLE
(*Yosenabe*)

Chicken, seafood and vegetables are combined in this hearty winter casserole and simmered in a richly-flavored stock. This dish is a particular favorite in the colder reaches of northern Japan.

INGREDIENTS (Serves 4)
4oz boned chicken, skin intact
4 large oysters, shucked
4 large hard-shelled clams, shucked
7oz tofu
½ package (4oz) shirataki noodles
7oz napa cabbage
1 medium carrot
2 leeks
4 large mushrooms, wiped and trimmed

STOCK
5 cups Dashi II
2 Tbsp soy sauce
2 Tbsp mirin
2 Tbsp sake
½ tsp salt

DIPPING SAUCE
ponzu sauce (see page 77)

CONDIMENTS
red maple radish (see page 77)
1 leek, shredded and rinsed (see "Cutting techniques", page 41)

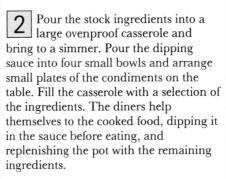

1 Cut the chicken into small chunks. Wash the oysters in lightly salted water, rinse and drain. Soak the clams in salted water and leave in a cool dark place until ready to use; then rinse under cold running water. Cut the *tofu* into 1in cubes. Parboil the *shirataki* for 1-2 minutes and drain. Wash and trim the vegetables. Slice the napa cabbage into 1in rounds. Cut the carrot into florettes (*see* page 43). Cut the leeks into 2in lengths. Remove the mushroom stems and cut a decorative cross in the top of each. Arrange all the ingredients attractively on a large platter.

2 Pour the stock ingredients into a large ovenproof casserole and bring to a simmer. Pour the dipping sauce into four small bowls and arrange small plates of the condiments on the table. Fill the casserole with a selection of the ingredients. The diners help themselves to the cooked food, dipping it in the sauce before eating, and replenishing the pot with the remaining ingredients.

ABOVE *A heavy ceramic casserole with a domed lid is the traditional container for mixed winter casserole. A flask of hot <u>sake</u> makes the perfect accompaniment.*

RICE AND RICE DISHES
Gohanmono

At the end of a Japanese meal, after a succession of rich and savory dishes, steaming white rice, pure and glistening, is served in delicate porcelain bowls. It is savored just as it is, accompanied by a few simple pickles. To the Japanese way of thinking, rice and food are one and the same, and one word *"gohan"* is used for both. Rice provides the true sustenance, and all the dishes which precede it are seen almost as an extended hors d'oeuvre. Nearly every meal in Japan, be it breakfast, lunch or dinner, ends with a bowl of rice. Many of the staples of the Japanese kitchen, such as *sake* and vinegar, and the bran used for pickling, are derived from rice.

The rice which is used in Japan is short-grained and white, not the long-grained variety used in Chinese and Indian cookery and more common in the West. Any short-grained rice may be used in Japanese recipes, although the Japanese themselves prefer Japanese rice. Rice is boiled or steamed until it is tender and moist and clings together, so that it is easy to eat with chopsticks. One is expected to finish every grain of rice in one's bowl, for it would be a crime to waste such a precious food.

COOKING RICE

Perfect rice, cooked the Japanese way, is white, fluffy and slightly sticky. Most Japanese kitchens contain an automatic rice cooker, which simply needs to be filled with rice and water in the correct proportions. It then boils and steams the rice, producing a perfect result every time, and keeps the rice hot and ready to eat all day long. Rice is served generally three times a day in Japan, making an automatic rice cooker almost a necessity for the busy Japanese housewife. Traditionally rice was cooked in a large saucepan and transferred to a wide flat wooden tub to serve.

INGREDIENTS (Serves 4)
1³/₄ cups short-grain white rice
2 cups water

1 Wash the rice well about 1 hour before cooking. Rinse several times and stir it with the hand until the rinsing water is clear. Combine with 2 cups fresh water and set aside to soak for at least 30 minutes.

2 Cover and bring to a boil over high heat. Reduce the heat to very low and simmer for 8-10 minutes. Turn off the heat and leave the pan on the cooker for another 15 minutes to steam. Do not lift the lid of the pot while the rice is cooking.

3 Dampen a wooden rice paddle or wooden spoon. Turn and fluff the rice with it before serving.

PORK CUTLET ON RICE
(Katsudon)

This very popular family lunch consists of a deep-fried breaded pork cutlet on a bowlful of hot rice, with an egg and onion topping. It makes a hearty meal in itself.

INGREDIENTS (Serves 4)
1³/₄ cups short-grain white rice
2 cups water
4 breaded pork cutlets (see recipe, page 112)
1 small onion
2 ¹/₂ cups Dashi II
¹/₂ cup mirin
¹/₃ cup soy sauce
6 eggs

1 Cook the rice in the water (*see* left). While the rice is cooking and resting, prepare the topping. Prepare and deep-fry the pork cutlets; drain on paper towels and slice diagonally into 1in strips. Set aside and keep warm.

2 Peel and slice the onion. Combine the *dashi, mirin* and soy sauce in a saucepan and bring to a boil. Add the onion and simmer until soft.

3 Lightly mix the eggs with chopsticks and slowly pour over the onion. Stir once when the egg is nearly set.

4 Half fill four large bowls with hot rice and neatly arrange a sliced breaded pork cutlet on each bowl. Before the egg is completely set, ladle a quarter of the egg mixture over each bowl, distributing all the liquid, and taking care that the egg mixture does not completely cover the cutlets.

CHICKEN AND EGG ON RICE
(*Oyako domburi*)

A favorite quick lunch in Japan consists of a big bowl of steaming rice topped with meat, fish or vegetables, often mixed with eggs. The tasty juices of the topping give added flavor to the rice. As all the ingredients may be prepared beforehand and simply heated and combined, this type of dish is a tasty way of using leftovers. This dish is usually served in a large deep bowl, like a cereal or deep soup bowl.

INGREDIENTS (*Serves 4*)
1¾ cups short-grain white rice
2 cups water
4oz boned chicken breast or thigh
4 leeks or scallions
4 dried mushrooms, reconstituted (see page 39)
2½ cups Dashi I
½ cup soy sauce
3 Tbsp mirin
1 Tbsp sugar
4 eggs

1 Cook the rice in the water (*see* page 156). Prepare the topping while the rice is cooking and resting. Cut the chicken into bite size pieces; cut the leeks or scallions diagonally into 2in lengths. Drain the mushrooms, cut off the stems, and finely slice the caps.

2 Prepare each portion separately. Measure out a quarter of the *dashi* into a small frying pan, and add a quarter of the chicken, and mushrooms. Bring to a boil and simmer for 5 minutes.

3 Add a quarter of the leeks or scallions and simmer for 1 more minute. Season with a quarter of the soy sauce, *mirin* and sugar.

4 Lightly mix the eggs with chopsticks and slowly pour a quarter of the egg mixture over the chicken and vegetables. Wait until the egg is half set, then stir only once.

5 Half fill a large bowl with hot rice and pour the egg mixture over the rice before the egg is fully set; the heat of the rice will continue to cook the egg. Make three more portions in the same way with the remaining ingredients.

CHESTNUT RICE
(*Kuri gohan*)

In Japan, chestnuts are used for both sweet and savory dishes. Chestnut rice is a classic fall dish. If fresh chestnuts are unobtainable, unsweetened bottled chestnuts, from Chinese and Japanese stores, may be used.

INGREDIENTS (Serves 4)
16 large fresh chestnuts
1³⁄₄ cups short-grain white rice
2 cups water
¹⁄₂ tsp salt

1 Soak the chestnuts overnight. With a sharp knife, pare away the peel and remove the inner skin. Neatly halve and soak in fresh water for another 3 or 4 hours.

2 Wash the rice thoroughly and soak for 1 hour. Place in a saucepan and add the water, chestnuts and salt. Cover, bring to a boil and simmer for 8-10 minutes. Turn off the heat and leave to steam for another 15 minutes. Serve, distributing the chestnuts evenly.

RICE WITH CHICKEN
(*Tori gohan*)

Chicken stock enriched with *sake* gives a rich flavor to the rice which is mixed with small pieces of chicken and dried mushroom.

INGREDIENTS (Serves 4)
1³⁄₄ cups short-grain white rice
4oz boned chicken breast or thigh
2 Tbsp soy sauce
4 dried mushrooms, reconstituted (see page 39)
2 cups chicken stock
4 tsp sake

4 sprigs fresh coriander

1 Wash the rice thoroughly and put in a strainer to drain for at least 30 minutes. Cut the chicken into short, ¹⁄₂in strips, sprinkle with the soy sauce and set aside to marinate for 30 minutes. Discard the mushroom stems and slice the caps finely.

2 Put the rice in a saucepan and pour the chicken stock and *sake* over it. Add the chicken and mushroom pieces. Bring to the boil over high heat, stirring occasionally. Cover tightly and reduce the heat to very low. Simmer for 8-10 minutes, then turn off the heat and leave, still covered, to steam for 15 minutes. Mix well and serve, garnishing each bowl with coriander leaf.

RICE WITH FIVE VEGETABLES
(Gomoku meshi)

Finely chopped vegetables, meat or fish are often cooked with the rice to color and flavor it. Rice cooked in this way is served instead of plain rice, usually for guests or special occasions.

INGREDIENTS (Serves 4)
1¾ cups short-grain white rice
½ medium carrot
½ burdock root
1 cake thin deep-fried tofu (aburage)
½ cake konnyaku (arum root)
4 dried mushrooms, reconstituted (see page 39)
4 Tbsp soy sauce
2 Tbsp sugar
2 cups Dashi II

1 Wash the rice thoroughly, drain and soak in fresh water for 1-2 hours. Prepare the five vegetables.

2 Scrape the carrot and burdock root. Douse the deep-fried *tofu* with boiling water to remove excess oil. Cut the carrot, *konnyaku* and deep-fried *tofu* into julienne strips.

3 Shred the burdock on the diagonal; place in cold water immediately. Remove the stems of the mushrooms and slice the caps finely.

4 Combine the soy sauce, sugar and *dashi* in a large bowl. Drain the burdock and add all five shredded vegetables to the *dashi*. Set aside for a few minutes to allow the flavors to mingle.

5 Drain the rice well and put into a saucepan. Pour the *dashi* together with the vegetables over the rice and stir well to mix. Bring to a boil, then cover tightly, reduce the heat to low and simmer for 10 minutes. Turn off the heat and leave the pan, still tightly covered, for another 15 minutes. Mix the rice with a wooden rice paddle or spoon to distribute the vegetables evenly before serving.

ABOVE *Finely chopped vegetables and chicken turn rice into a festive dish — chestnut rice (top right), rice with chicken (middle left) and rice with five vegetables.*

VINEGARED RICE FOR SUSHI
(*Sushi meshi*)

Vinegared rice is the basis for a wide variety of dishes which go under the general name of *sushi*, consisting usually of raw fish or crisp vegetables. To make vinegared rice, sweetened vinegar is added to freshly cooked rice in a shallow wooden tub, and the rice is tossed and fanned at the same time, so that each grain remains separate and cools as quickly as possible, resulting in a glossy sheen. To make 7oz vinegared rice, simply halve the quantities of ingredients and follow the instructions below.

INGREDIENTS (Serves 4)
1¾ cups short-grain white rice
2 cups water
4 Tbsp rice vinegar
2 Tbsp sugar
2 tsp salt

1 Cook the rice in the water (*see* page 156). Cool to room temperature. When the rice has rested, place in a wide shallow container.

2 Combine the vinegar, sugar and salt and heat to dissolve the sugar and salt. Sprinkle the rice with the vinegar mixture.

3 Quickly and lightly cut and toss the rice with a wooden rice paddle or spoon. Ideally, you should fan the rice as you toss it, so that it becomes glossy. Vinegared rice should be used immediately. Otherwise cover with a damp cloth and use within a few hours.

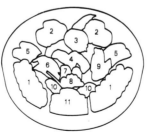

Salmon roe with paper thin cucumber slices. (10) Ark shell. (11) Spiral rolled thick sushi with rolled omelet strips, cucumber, gourd strips and dried mushroom.

ABOVE *Sushi arranged with thick and thin sushi rolls on a large platter. (1) Thin rolled sushi with pickles and cucumber. (2) Thick rolled sushi with dried mushrooms, cucumber, gourd strips and rolled cucumber strips. (3) Squid rose. (4) Yellowtail. (5) Tuna. (6) Squid. (7) Octopus. (8) Cucumber slices. (9)*

THICK SUSHI ROLLS
(Futomaki)

Sushi rolls are one of Japan's favorite foods, to be found all over Japan, in every kind of store—from tiny wayside stalls deep in the countryside to exclusive stores in fashionable Ginza. Morsels of different vegetables and other tidbits cluster together in a multicolor design against a background of gleaming white rice, the whole wrapped in dark green seaweed. The rolls taste as appealing as they look, and tend to be eaten as a treat or a snack. A bamboo rolling mat is helpful in making *sushi* rolls.

INGREDIENTS (Serves 4)
vinegared rice made from 1 cup uncooked rice
2 cakes dried tofu (koya dofu)
2 dried gourd strips, each 12in long
4 dried mushrooms
3½ cups Dashi II
3 Tbsp soy sauce
3 Tbsp sugar
2 Tbsp mirin
½ cucumber, 6in long
2 sheets nori seaweed
1 tsp rice vinegar
3 Tbsp water

1 Prepare the vinegared rice (*see* page 162). Soak the dried *tofu* in hot water for a few minutes, then squeeze, and repeat until the water which is squeezed out is clear. Reconstitute the gourd strips and mushrooms (*see* page 39). Put the dried *tofu* in a saucepan with 2 cups *dashi*, 1 Tbsp soy sauce and 1 Tbsp sugar. Combine the gourd strips with 1¼ cups *dashi* and 1 Tbsp each soy sauce, *mirin* and sugar. Remove the mushroom stems and slice the caps finely; combine the caps with ¼ cup *dashi* and 1 Tbsp each soy sauce, *mirin* and sugar.

2 Bring each of the three mixtures to the boil and simmer for 20 minutes, until the simmering liquid is nearly absorbed. Leave to cool in the simmering liquid, then drain. Slice each cake of dried *tofu* into six strips. Slice the cucumber into narrow strips and set aside in lightly salted water to soak for 20 minutes. Drain and pat dry with paper towels. This can all be done beforehand.

3 Toast the *nori* by waving it over a high flame for a few seconds until it changes color and becomes fragrant. Lay on a bamboo rolling mat. Combine the vinegar and water and use to keep your fingers moistened. Place half the vinegared rice on the *nori*.

4 Keeping your fingers moist, spread the rice to cover three-quarters of the *nori*, extending right to the edges.

5 Spread half the dried *tofu*, gourd strips, mushrooms and cucumber in a thick strip across the rice.

6 Holding the ingredients in place with your fingers, begin to roll firmly, using your thumbs to roll up the bamboo mat. Try to keep the ingredients in the center of the roll.

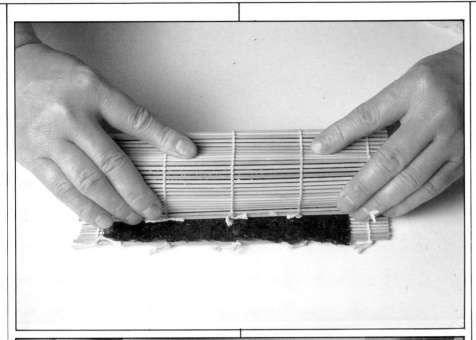

7 Continue rolling, taking care not to trap the bamboo mat inside the roll.

8 Complete the roll and gently but firmly press the mat around the roll for a few seconds to shape it. Unroll. Wet a sharp knife and cut the roll in half. Then cut each half into four slices. Repeat with the remaining ingredients.

THIN SUSHI ROLLS
(Hosomaki)

One of the most popular dishes in a *sushi* bar is thin *sushi* rolls, always neatly served in groups of six, consisting of a filling such as cucumber, raw tuna or bright pink or yellow pickle slices, rolled in vinegared rice and *nori* seaweed. Nowadays all manner of fillings may appear in these rolls; avocado, totally unknown in Japan, is said to be a favorite in Californian *sushi* bars. *Takuan* pickle and cucumber, together with strips of dried *tofu* and gourd strips, prepared as for thick *sushi* rolls, are the traditional fillings.

INGREDIENTS (Serves 4)
vinegared rice made from 1 cup uncooked rice
¼ cup <u>takuan</u> pickle
½ cucumber, 6in long
2 sheets <u>nori</u> seaweed
1 tsp rice vinegar, mixed with 3 Tbsp water
freshly-made <u>wasabi</u> horseradish (see <u>sashimi</u> section, page 76)

1 Prepare the vinegared rice (*see* page 162). Shred the *takuan* pickle. Slice the cucumber into narrow strips. Toast the *nori* by moving it over a flame for a few seconds until it changes color and becomes fragrant, and halve each sheet of *nori* with scissors.

2 To make the takuan pickle rolls, lay one half sheet of *nori* on the bamboo rolling mat. Moisten your hands with the vinegar, place one-fourth of the vinegared rice on the *nori* and spread to cover the edges, leaving the top 1in uncovered. Lay half the *takuan* pickle in a line along the center of the rice.

3 Holding the *takuan* in place with your fingers, roll up the bamboo mat to form a firm roll. Press the mat around the roll to shape it, remove the mat and with a sharp knife cut the roll into six slices, cutting either diagonally or straight downward. Repeat with the *takuan*.

4 To make cucumber rolls, lay a sheet of *nori* on the bamboo mat and spread over a quarter of the rice. Smear a thin line of *wasabi* horseradish along the center of the rice, and lay one or two strips of cucumber on the *wasabi*. Roll up and cut as before.

LEFT *An assortment of thick and thin <u>sushi</u> rolls makes a colorful and delicious dish.*

SUSHI ON RICE, TOKYO-STYLE
(*Chirashi zushi edo mae*)

This simple way to assemble *sushi*, consisting of raw fish and vegetables arranged on a bed of vinegared rice, is often prepared at home. The ingredients may be literally scattered (*"chirashi"*) on a large bowl of rice, or, for a more festive effect, each portion may be artistically arranged in small lacquered wooden boxes.

INGREDIENTS (Serves 4)
vinegared rice made from 1 cup uncooked rice
1 sheet nori seaweed
1lb fresh raw fish (shrimps, squid, tuna, salmon, salmon roe, etc)
¼ cucumber

ROLLED OMELET
2 eggs, plus 1 egg yolk
4 Tbsp Dashi II
1 tsp mirin
¼ tsp salt

1 lemon
soy sauce
1 tsp freshly made wasabi horseradish (see page 76)

1 Prepare the vinegared rice (*see* page 162). Lightly toast the *nori* seaweed. Clean, fillet and slice the fish into ¼in thick slices (*see* page 73). Cut the cucumber into four "fans" (*see* page 43, "Cutting techniques"). Prepare one rolled omelet using the above ingredients (following the recipe on page 98). Cut two thin slices from the lemon and halve to form half moons. Pour some soy sauce into four small dipping bowls. Put a dab of freshly made *wasabi* horseradish in each.

2 Spread the rice in four individual containers or one large bowl. With scissors, cut the *nori* into thin strips and scatter over the rice. Dab a little *wasabi* horseradish in the center of each slice of fish and arrange the fish slices artistically to cover the rice.

3 Garnish the dish with four cucumber "fans" and four half moons of lemon.

4 Slice the rolled omelet into ½in rectangular slices and halve two slices to make triangles. Garnish the dish with the four triangles of omelet.

ABOVE *Sushi* with rice (top right) is often neatly arranged in a lacquered wooden box, and served with soy sauce containing a little *wasabi* horseradish (top left). Golden *sushi* pouches (bottom left) are a popular and nourishing snack or quick meal.

1 Prepare the vinegared rice (*see* page 162). Pour boiling water over the deep-fried *tofu* cakes to remove oil; when cool enough to handle, halve each cake across. Ease each half open to make 8 pouches. Reconstitute the gourd strips (*see* page 39). Combine the *tofu* pouches and gourd strips with the simmering stock ingredients in a saucepan and bring to a boil. Cover with a drop lid and simmer for 20 minutes. Leave to cool in the simmering stock. Remove the *tofu* pouches and gourd ribbon, squeeze and drain. Parboil and shred the carrot.

2 Mix the rice with the shredded carrot. With moistened hands pick up a small ball of rice and shape into an oval.

3 Open a *tofu* pouch and gently slide the rice ball into the pouch. Fold the sides and then the top flap of the pouch over the rice to close it. Fill all the *tofu* pouches in the same way.

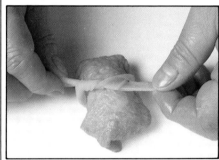

4 Cut the prepared gourd strips in half and use to tie four *tofu* pouches.

GOLDEN SUSHI POUCHES
(Inari sushi)

Deep-fried *tofu* stuffed with vinegared rice makes a tasty and nutritious lunch or snack. Tiny shreds of carrot color and flavor the rice, but these may be replaced by bamboo shoot or lotus root prepared in the same way.

INGREDIENTS (Serves 4)
vinegared rice made from 1 cup uncooked rice
4 cakes deep-fried tofu (aburage)
2 dried gourd strips, each 12in long

SIMMERING STOCK
3 Tbsp mirin
3 Tbsp sugar
4 Tbsp soy sauce
1¼ cups Dashi II

¼ carrot
salt

SUSHI
(Nigiri sushi)

Sushi, slices of fresh raw fish on slabs of vinegared rice, is quite addictive. Japan is full of *sushi* bars, from cheap self-service cafes where plates of ready-made *sushi* roll past you on a conveyor belt, to bars where glowingly fresh slabs of fish are sliced before your very eyes and deftly combined with rice in a few seconds. In Japan, *sushi*-making is usually left to the professionals; however, it is not difficult to make your own. Use only the freshest raw fish, and prepare the *sushi* just before eating. Custom decrees that it should always be served in pairs.

Sushi is usually eaten with the fingers; turn it over so that the fish is underneath and dip the fish in soy sauce before eating. Mixed *sushi* can be served as part of a meal, or as the meal itself, followed by *miso* soup.

INGREDIENTS (Serves 4-6)
vinegared rice made from 1 cup uncooked rice
1lb fresh raw fish (tuna, shrimps, salmon, squid, etc)
1 tsp freshly made <u>wasabi</u> horseradish (see page 76)
1 tsp rice vinegar mixed with 3 Tbsp water
soy sauce

1 Prepare the vinegared rice (*see* page 162). Clean, fillet and slice the fish into ⅛in thick slices (*see sashimi,* page 73). Prepare the *wasabi* horseradish.

2 Keeping your hands moistened with the vinegar mixture, dab a little *wasabi* horseradish in the center of a slice of fish.

3 Form a small ball of rice in your fingers and quickly shape into a rectangle. Press onto the slice of fish.

4 Press the rice and fish together with both hands to firm and neaten the rectangle. Carefully set aside. Continue to make the fish and rice rectangles in the same way until all the ingredients are used.

ABOVE *Mixed sushi (<u>nigiri-sushi</u>), served in deep trays of lacquered wood, is an essential part of special dinners and festive gatherings.*

NOODLES
Menrui

Noodles come in many shapes, sizes and colors. White wheat noodles may be round, or flat and wide, or very fine. There are also gray narrow buckwheat noodles, yellow noodles and even green noodles, colored with green tea. Noodles represent the hearty folk cuisine of Japan, and are never included in a formal meal. Anyone in search of a quick, cheap and nourishing meal will very probably go to a noodle shop, for there are more noodles shops than any other kind of restaurant in Japan. You can even devour a steaming bowl of noodles standing up in the station.

Noodles are always served in stock, in a hot soup in winter and chilled—with a highly flavored dipping sauce—in summer. They make a delicious meal at any time of the year.

Noodle connoisseurs prefer to eat their noodles with the minimum of stock, so as to savor the subtle taste of the noodles themselves. It is a sign of enjoyment to slurp one's noodles, particularly if they are hot. The following noodle recipes may be made using either buckwheat or wheat noodles.

COOKING NOODLES

Noodles are always cooked *al dente*, that is, they are cooked through to the center but are removed from the water when still quite firm. White wheat noodles *(udon)* are cooked as we cook spaghetti, in plenty of rapidly boiling salted water, for about 10 minutes, until just cooked. Buckwheat noodles *(soba)* may be cooked in the same way, but here is the traditional Japanese way of cooking buckwheat noodles.

INGREDIENTS (Serves 4)
14oz dried buckwheat noodles

1 Bring plenty of unsalted water to a rolling boil in a large deep saucepan. Gradually add the noodles. Stir slowly to stop the noodles from sticking. When the water returns to the boil, add ½ cup cold water. Bring back to a boil and repeat. When the water boils a third time, lower the heat and simmer for 2-3 minutes until the noodles are just cooked.

2 Drain the noodles and immerse in cold water, stirring gently to separate the strands and remove starch. Place the noodles in a strainer and immerse in hot water to reheat before using.

BUCKWHEAT NOODLES IN HOT BROTH
(Kake soba)

Buckwheat noodles originated in the colder northern parts of Japan, and are particularly popular in Tokyo and the north. They are usually served quite simply so that the delicate taste of the noodle itself can be appreciated.

INGREDIENTS (Serves 4)
14oz dried buckwheat noodles

NOODLE BROTH
3½ cups Dashi II
3 Tbsp dark soy sauce
2 Tbsp sugar
2 Tbsp mirin
2 tsp salt

2 young leeks or scallions

1 Cook the noodles (*see* page 172). Combine the noodle broth ingredients and bring to a boil; keep warm. Shred and rinse the leeks or scallions (*see* "Cutting techniques", page 41). Warm four deep bowls. Immerse the noodles in a strainer in boiling water for a few seconds to reheat. Divide among the four bowls.

2 Ladle the hot broth over the noodles and top with a mound of shredded leek or scallion.

ABOVE *Buckwheat noodles in hot broth (kake sobba) is usually served with minimal decoration (top). Chilled buckwheat noodles (mori soba) is a popular summer dish (bottom).*

CHILLED BUCKWHEAT NOODLES
(*Mori soba*)

In summer buckwheat noodles are served chilled in slatted bamboo containers, and dipped into a tangy dipping sauce into which *wasabi* horseradish and shredded leek are mixed.

INGREDIENTS (Serves 4)
14oz dried buckwheat noodles

DIPPING SAUCE
2½ cups Dashi II
½ cup dark soy sauce
4 Tbsp mirin
1 tsp sugar

2 young leeks or scallions
1 tsp freshly made wasabi horseradish (see page 76)
½ sheet nori seaweed

1 Cook the noodles (*see* page 172). Combine the dipping sauce ingredients and bring to a boil; chill. Shred and rinse the leeks or scallions (*see* page 41), and prepare the *washabi* horseradish. Toast the *nori* seaweed and cut with scissors into thin strips.

2 Divide the chilled dipping sauce among four small bowls. Mound portions of leeks and *wasabi* in four small containers. Put the drained cold noodles in four containers or plates and scatter strips of *nori* seaweed over each portion.

NOODLES IN SMALL CASEROLES
(*Nabe yaki udon*)

Traditionally, this hearty winter dish is prepared and served in individual earthenware casseroles.

INGREDIENTS (Serves 4)
14oz dried udon noodles
4oz boned chicken, skin intact
1 tsp each soy sauce and sake
1 cake kamaboko (fish cake)
4 dried mushrooms, reconstituted (see page 39)

SIMMERING STOCK
½ cup Dashi II
1 Tbsp each soy sauce, mirin and sugar

4 scallions
4 pieces prawn tempura (see tempura recipe, page 116)

NOODLE BROTH
5 cups Dashi II
4 Tbsp light soy sauce
3 Tbsp mirin
½ tsp salt

4 eggs

1 Cook the noodles (*see* page 172). Cut the chicken into small chunks, sprinkle with soy sauce and *sake* and set aside for 10 minutes to marinate. Cut the *kamaboko* into ¼in slices. Remove the mushroom stems and cut a decorative cross in the top of each mushroom cap. Combine with the simmering stock ingredients and simmer for 15 minutes. Slice the green part of the scallions on the diagonal into 2in slices. Prepare the prawn *tempura*. Combine the noodle broth ingredients and bring to a boil; keep warm.

2 Put the noodles into four small ovenproof casseroles with lids. Divide the chicken, *kamaboko*, mushrooms and scallions among the four casseroles; ladle the noodle broth over them.

3 Cover the casseroles and bring to a boil; carefully scoop off any foam.

4 With the back of a spoon make a small hollow in the noodles in each casserole and break an egg into the hollow. Immediately cover the casserole and turn off the heat; the egg will semi-set. Add a piece of prawn *tempura* to each casserole and serve immediately.

"MOON VIEWING" NOODLES
(*Tsukimi udon*)

Fat white *udon* noodles, made from wheat, are particularly popular in Osaka and southern Japan, where they are served in a pale broth. Admiring the full moon is a traditional activity in fall, and in this dish the egg yolk in each bowl of noodles resembles a perfect full moon.

INGREDIENTS (Serves 4)
14oz dried *udon* noodles

NOODLE BROTH
5 cups *Dashi II*
2 Tbsp light soy sauce
2 tsp salt
1 Tbsp sugar
2 tsp *sake*

4 scallions
½ sheet *nori*
4 eggs

1 Cook the noodles in plenty of rapidly boiling salted water for 10 minutes, until just cooked. Drain and immerse in cold water, stirring gently to separate the strands. Drain and set aside.

2 Combine the noodle broth ingredients and bring to a boil; keep warm. Slice the green part of the scallions on the diagonal into 2in slices. Toast the *nori* and cut with scissors into rectangles 1 × 2in.

3 Warm four deep bowls. Put the noodles in a strainer and immerse in boiling water for a few seconds to reheat; divide among the four bowls and top with slices of scallions. Gently break an egg onto each bowl of noodles, taking care not to break the yolk. Immediately ladle the hot broth over the noodles; the hot broth will slightly cook the egg.

4 Garnish each bowl with *nori* and serve immediately.

ABOVE *Fox noodles (kitsune udon) is a combination of noodles and deep-fried tofu (left). "Moon viewing" noodles (tsukimi udon) is a popular dish in southern Japan.*

FOX NOODLES
(*Kitsune udon*)

The wily fox, who figures widely in Japanese folklore, is said to be extremely partial to deep-fried *tofu*, and this hearty dish of noodles and deep-fried *tofu* would be very much to his taste.

INGREDIENTS (Serves 4)
14oz dried <u>udon</u> *noodles*

NOODLE BROTH
5 cups <u>Dashi II</u>
2 Tbsp light soy sauce
2 tsp salt
1 Tbsp sugar
2 tsp <u>sake</u>

2 scallions
4 cakes thin deep-fried <u>tofu</u> *(*<u>aburage</u>*)*

SIMMERING STOCK
1 cup <u>Dashi II</u>
2 Tbsp soy sauce
1 Tbsp sugar

1 Cook the noodles (*see* page 172). Combine the noodle broth ingredients and bring to a boil; keep warm. Shred and rinse the scallions (*see* page 41).

2 Pour boiling water over the deep-fried *tofu* to remove oil. Drain and combine with the simmering ingredients in a small saucepan and bring to a boil. Cover with a drop lid and simmer for 10 minutes.

3 Warm four deep bowls. Put the noodles in a strainer and immerse in boiling water for a few seconds to reheat; divide among the four bowls Arrange one folded cake of deep-fried *tofu* and a quarter of the scallion on each bowl, ladle the hot broth over them and serve.

PICKLES
Tsukemono

The characteristic flavor of Japan lies not in all its rich and complex dishes so much as in the humble and much loved pickles which are served with the rice at the end of the meal. A bowl of rice and a small dish of different types of crunchy pickles are often served to make a simple and satisfying breakfast or lunch; and pickles, with their nostalgic flavor of rural Japan, are what the exiled Japanese yearns for most.

Pickles are an essential accompaniment to rice, and every Japanese kitchen contains a store of pickles, some bought and some home-made, so that several different pickles can be served at each meal. Every area in Japan produces distinctive pickles, and an enormous variety of fine ready-made pickles can be bought not only in Japan but also in Japanese stores and some Chinese supermarkets in the West.

Many simple pickles can be easily and quickly made at home. The main pickling medium used in Japan, particularly for commercial pickles, is rice bran *nuka*. Whole vegetables such as napa cabbage and *daikon* radish are hung from the eaves to dry and then buried in rice bran in wooden barrels for 2–3 weeks. For home pickling, salt, *miso*, *sake* lees and rice vinegar are frequently used. Almost any raw vegetable can be pickled; napa cabbage, *daikon* radish, eggplant, turnip and cucumber are the most popular.

A variety of pickles of contrasting colors and types should be served at a meal. Rinse the pickle first, and if it is very salty you may need to soak it in cold water for a few minutes. Then dry the pickles with paper towels, chop into bite size pieces and serve on small individual plates. A drop of soy sauce may be used to flavor the pickles before eating.

SWEET PICKLED GINGER
(Sushoga)

Ginger pickled in sweetened vinegar makes a deliciously tart yet sweet pickle which is invariably served with *sushi*. The ginger naturally turns a little pink in the marinade. In Japan pickled plum juice is sometimes added to give a richer red; red food coloring could also be used. If you can find young ginger shoots, prepare them in the same way to make a delicious pickle which is frequently served with grilled fish.

INGREDIENTS (Serves 4)
½ cup fresh ginger root
2–3 tsp salt
½ cup rice vinegar
3 Tbsp water
1 Tbsp sugar
a little pickled plum juice or red food coloring (optional)

1 Wash the ginger thoroughly, peeling away any discolored skin. Sprinkle lightly with salt, put into a bowl or jar, cover and set aside for 1–2 days.

2 Drain the ginger and put in a clean glass or ceramic bowl or jar. Combine the vinegar, water and sugar (and red coloring if required) in a small saucepan, bring to the boil and pour over the ginger. Cover the bowl or jar and set aside for at least 7 days. To serve, cut paper thin slices of ginger along the grain and serve a little on individual plates. Sweet pickled ginger will keep for several months in the refrigerator.

MIXED VEGETABLES PICKLED IN SAKE

These tasty mixed pickles are very quick to make and can be prepared just before the meal. Make in a bowl and press using a wooden drop lid or a plate which fits neatly inside the bowl on top of the pickles, topped with a weight such as a jar of water.

INGREDIENTS (Serves 4)
4 leaves napa cabbage
4 leaves red cabbage
1 small turnip
½ cucumber
1 medium carrot
3 Tbsp raisins
salt
½ cup sake

1 Wash and trim the vegetables. Cut the napa cabbage and red cabbage into small 1 x 1in pieces. Halve the turnip and slice into half moons. Cut the cucumber into small chunks and cut the carrot into sticks. Chop the raisins coarsely. Carefully pat the chopped vegetables dry with paper towels.

2 Place the vegetables in a glass or ceramic bowl and sprinkle with salt, stirring to ensure that all the vegetables are salted. Set aside for 10 minutes.

3 Knead the vegetables and squeeze to press out as much water as possible.

4 Place the vegetables in a clean ceramic bowl and mix in the raisins. Sprinkle over the *sake*. Set a drop lid or plate on the vegetables and top with a weight. Set aside for about 20 minutes. Drain and rinse the vegetables and serve small quantities on individual dishes.

SALT PICKLED VEGETABLES
(*Shiozuke*)

Salt pickling is a very common way of pickling vegetables; napa cabbage *daikon* radish and cucumber all make crisp and delicious salt pickles. The quality of the salt affects the quality of these pickles, so use pure sea salt or coarse salt for the best flavor.

INGREDIENTS *(Serves 4)*
1 napa cabbage
   or 2 cucumbers
   or 2 daikon radishes
3 Tbsp salt

1 Wash and trim the vegetables. napa cabbage: cut off the base of the cabbage and cut the cabbage lengthways into six or eight pieces. Cut each piece into 2in chunks. Cucumber: peel and seed the cucumbers and cut into 1/2in slices. *Daikon* radish: peel, quarter and cut into 2in lengths. Lightly pat the vegetables with paper towels to dry.

2 Layer the chopped vegetables with salt in a large glass or ceramic bowl, beginning and ending with a layer of salt. Cover with a drop lid or plate slightly smaller than the top of the bowl, and top with a weight such as a jar of water.

3 Leave the bowl in a cool dark place for 3–4 days. The brine will quickly rise above the level of the vegetables.

4 To serve, remove the required quantity of pickled vegetable from the bowl; rinse, squeeze and cut into small pieces. Serve in small quantities of pickle in individual dishes. The pickles may be flavored with a drop of soy sauce to taste. The remaining pickles will keep for 2–3 months in the brine.

PICKLED EGGPLANT
(*Nasu no shoyuzuke*)

Deep purple eggplant pickles are particulary popular. Small Japanese eggplants may be pickled in a number of ways, and are sometimes pickled whole and then buried in *miso* for as long as 6 months. Here is a quick eggplant pickle.

INGREDIENTS *(Serves 4)*
16oz eggplants
2 Tbsp salt
3¾ cups water
3 Tbsp soy sauce
3 Tbsp mirin
3 Tbsp sugar
1 tsp wasabi, freshly prepared

1 Wash and trim the eggplants and cut into thick slices. Dissolve the salt in the water, and soak the eggplants for 1–2 hours. Drain, lightly squeeze and place in a clean jar or bowl.

2 Blend the remaining ingredients and pour over the eggplant slices, turning the eggplants so that all surfaces are covered. Cover and refrigerate for 3 hours, turning occasionally.

3 To serve, drain the required amount of eggplant slices and cut into small pieces. Serve on individual plates.

FRUIT
Kudamono

At the end of a Japanese meal, when all the dishes are cleared away, tiny portions of fresh fruit are served after a brief respite. The fruit, a coda to the meal, is prepared with as much care as the meal itself. With a few precise strokes of the knife, the chef transforms apples, pears or oranges into minor works of art—delicate flowers, petals or even small baskets. Each guest receives a mere mouthful of fruit, set on an elegant plate, to be eaten never with the fingers but with a tiny fork or toothpick.

Japan has a relatively cool climate and the fruits which most frequently appear on Japanese tables are hardy fruits—apples and crisp round pears from Hokkaido in the north, persimmons from central Japan and mandarin oranges from the south—firm bodied fruits that lend themselves to decorative cutting. Soft fruits such as strawberries are usually washed, trimmed and served whole, with a small fork or toothpick. Grapes are always carefully peeled. Nowadays many imported fruits are available in Japan, and they too are always exquisitely carved and arranged.

Fruit should always be cut just before serving. A good sharp knife is essential for fruit cutting.

ORANGES *(Mikan)*

Oranges are a popular fruit in Japan. Decorative cutting techniques make use of the strenth of the skin, which retains its shape, making forms such as orange baskets possible.

ZIGZAG ORANGE HALVES

1 Wash and dry the orange and level off the base. Cut the orange in a zigzag all the way around, cutting right through to the center.

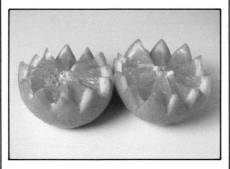

2 Gently ease apart the two halves of the orange. One half is one serving

ORANGE BASKETS

Orange baskets are traditionally served at the festival to give thanks for baby girls, which takes place on March 3rd. This is a very attractive way to serve oranges. Allow one orange per person.

1 Wash and dry the orange and level off the base. Set the orange on its base and make two parallel cuts downward, about 1/2in apart, to form the handle, cutting through the top third of the orange. Make two horizontal cuts from the sides of the orange to meet the vertical cuts, forming the top of the basket.

2 Remove the two segments. Slide the knife under the handle and neatly remove the flesh. Carefully remove as much of the flesh of the orange as possible, keeping the flesh in large chunks. The remaining orange skin will now be in the form of a basket. Neatly chop the flesh and pile into the basket, filling it just to the rim.

ABOVE *(clockwise) Zigzag orange halves; orange baskets; apple petals; harlequin apple, and banana mountain peaks.*

APPLES *(Ringo)*

Apples, with their firm texture and contrasting white flesh and colorful red or green skin, are the ideal fruit for decorative cutting. Choose apples for their visual quality rather than their flavor, and look for large crisp apples with a flawless skin.

HARLEQUIN APPLE

1 Wash and trim the apple and level off the base. Neatly score the skin in a zigzag all the way around the apple.

2 Carefully pare away the skin with a single stroke between each point, so that the remaining white flesh is neatly contoured.

APPLE PETALS

This is perhaps the most popular fruit cutting technique of all. A few simple strokes of the knife transform the apple.

1 Choose a large, firm, white fleshed apple; one large apple will be sufficient for four to six people. Wash and dry the apple and slice it neatly in half.

2 Divide the apple into sixths or eighths, depending on the size of the apple. Make a straight cut down the inside of each segment to remove the core.

3 Make two very shallow diagonal cuts through the skin of the apple, meeting in the center of the segment. With a paring motion, slide the knife between the skin and flesh of the apple to the point where the two diagonal cuts meet, releasing the central diamond of skin.

4 Remove and discard the central diamond, leaving two red petals.

5 Prepare a green apple in the same way, making four instead of two petals, and arrange one or two apple segments of each color on small plates. This technique is also used for oranges and pears.

BANANAS *(BANANA)*

Long narrow fruits such as bananas are cut into mountain peaks. Cut the banana just before serving to avoid discoloration.

BANANA MOUNTAIN PEAKS

1 Trim the end of the banana and make a lengthways cut halfway through the fruit.

2 Leave the knife in the banana as a guide and with a second knife make a diagonal cut through to the center.

3 Turn the banana and repeat on the other side. Separate the two halves to make mountain peaks, and arrange two halves decoratively on one plate for a single serving.

CAKES & SWEETS
Okashi

In Japan cakes and sweets are not traditionally served after a meal. However, the Japanese are every bit as sweet toothed as Westerners. Whenever a guest comes to visit, tea and a cake or sweet is invariably served. The cake is eaten before, rather than with, the tea to sweeten the palate before drinking the unsweetened green tea, and is small and extremely sweet. A few simple cakes are made at home but by and large Japanese housewives buy exquisitely shaped and colored little cakes from speciality shops. Cakes are made from a variety of materials, including of course sugar, and also *aduki* beans, glutinous rice, *agar* (a seaweed-based gelling agent) and seasonal ingredients such as chestnuts. Baking is not a traditional Japanese cooking method, and cakes are usually steamed, simmered, deep fried or set with *agar*. Cakes bought from shops are always exquisite and vary with the seasons, being shaped into plum blossoms in the spring, maple leaves and chestnuts in the fall, and all manner of delicate natural forms such as nightingales. Cakes are admired for their appearance rather than for their taste. One or two morsels of cake make one serving, and are neatly arranged on a plate or a folded sheet of hand-made paper, with a tiny fork or toothpick to cut and eat them.

There are two types of Japanese cakes. Hard cakes *(higashi)* are made largely of sugar and are invariably purchased; they are considered to be more suitable for summer. Soft cakes *(namagashi)* are sometimes made at home, and need to be eaten while they are fresh. They are made from a variety of ingredients and usually include sweet bean paste.

JELLIED PEACHES
(Momo no kenten)

Agar combined with puréed peach makes a refreshing gelatin which is served in summer with iced tea. Stored in the refrigerator it will keep for 2–3 days.

INGREDIENTS (Serves 8)
1 stick *agar (kanten)*
2 cups water
1½ cups sugar
½ cup fresh peach pulp
2 Tbsp fresh lemon juice
2 egg whites

1 Rinse the *agar* and soak in cold water for 20 minutes. Then squeeze and tear into small pieces. Combine with the measured water in a saucepan and bring slowly to a boil. Simmer, stirring occasionally, until the *agar* dissolves.

2 Add the sugar and continue to simmer, stirring, until the sugar has dissolved.

3 Line a fine sieve with cheesecloth and strain the *agar* mixture through it into a bowl. Stir in the peach pulp and lemon juice and leave to cool.

4 Beat the egg whites until stiff, and gradually fold in the cooled peach mixture. Pour into a straight-sided square or rectangular tin and refrigerate until set. Cut into 1in squares or diamonds and serve one or two on small plates.

SWEET BEAN GELATIN (Yokan)

Sweet bean gelatin is one of the most popular sweets, and is frequently made at home. Two or three slices, carefully arranged on a small plate, make a pleasant accompaniment to tea. *Agar*, the gelling agent, is derived from a seaweed and makes a more finely textured gelatin than gelatine. You will need a square or rectangular container, about 6in square, for setting the gelatin. The following quantities will produce enough for about eight portions.

INGREDIENTS
½ stick *agar (kanten)*
1¼ cups water
2 cups sweet bean paste
sugar (optional)
¼ tsp salt

1 Rinse the *agar* and soak in cold water for 20 minutes. Then squeeze the *agar* and tear into small pieces. Combine with the measured water in a saucepan and bring slowly to the boil. Simmer, stirring occasionally, until the *agar* dissolves.

2 Add the sweet bean paste and sugar and boil for 3 minutes, stirring continuously with a wooden spoon. Stir in the salt and remove from the heat. Allow to cool slightly.

3 Pour into a straight-sided square or rectangular container about 6in square and set aside to cool and set. Refrigerate the tin to speed up this process.

4 Cut the gelatin into oblongs ½×½in and serve on small plates.

SWEET BEAN SOUP WITH RICE CAKES (*Zenzai*)

This thick sweet soup with a sticky rice cake in each bowl is a favorite Japanese winter snack.

INGREDIENTS (Serves 4)
½ cup <u>aduki</u> beans
½ cup sugar
¼ tsp salt
4 rice cakes

1 Wash the beans and put in a large saucepan with water to cover. Bring to a boil, then drain and discard water. Cover again with water, bring back to a boil, then reduce heat and simmer for 1-1½ hours until the beans are soft.

2 Add the sugar and enough water to make a thick soupy consistency. Simmer over medium heat for 15 minutes, stirring frequently.

3 Broil the rice cakes under a hot broiler or over a hot flame, turning once so that the cakes do not burn, until both sides are crisp and brown.

4 Put one rice cake in each of four deep bowls and ladle over the hot soup. The rice cakes should be eaten with chopsticks; the soup is then drunk directly from the bowl.

SWEET BEAN PASTE (*Anko*)

Sweet bean paste is the basis for most Japanese home-made cakes. It is made from *aduki* beans which are cooked until soft and then sweetened. The beans may be lightly mashed and left as a chunky paste, or puréed and strained to make a smooth paste. Sweet bean paste should be freshly made and immediately used in a sweet or cake recipe.

INGREDIENTS to make 2½ cups paste
½ cup <u>aduki</u> beans
½ cup sugar
¼ tsp salt

1 Wash the beans and put in a large saucepan with water to cover. Bring to a boil, then drain and discard water. Cover again with water, bring back to a boil, then reduce heat and simmer for 1-1½ hours until the beans are soft.

2 Drain. Put the beans in a sieve over a bowl of clean water and rub them through the sieve so that the skins remain in the sieve and the pulp is strained into the water. (Omit this step to make chunky bean paste.) Discard the skins.

3 Pour the pulp and water through a piece of cheesecloth or fine cotton cloth. Gather the cheesecloth around the pulp and squeeze out as much water as possible.

4 Combine the pulp and sugar in a saucepan and heat over very low heat, moving the mixture back and forth with a wooden spoon until the mixture is glossy and thick. Add the salt and set aside. Leave covered in a cool place until ready to use.

LEFT *Most Japanese home-made hard cakes (higashi) are basically made from sweet bean paste (anko). These hard cakes (top) are beautifully presented in a box topped by two Japanese dolls. Sweet bean gelatine (yokan) is a very popular sweet (bottom), and is easy to make at home.*

Useful addresses

JAPANESE FOOD STORES IN THE UNITED STATES

NORTHERN CALIFORINIA

ABC Fish and Oriental Food
1911 Portrero Way
Sacramento 95822

Asahi Market
5616 Thornton Ave.
Newark 94560

Asahi Ya
229 East Alpine Ave.
Stockton 95009

Dobashi Company
240 E. Jackson St.
San Jose 95112

International Market
2019 Fillmore St.
San Francisco 94115

Kenson Trading
1251 Stockton St.
San Francisco 94133

Miko's Japanese Foods
524 Tuolumne
Vallejo 94590

Nishioka Fish Market
665 N. Sixth St.
San Jose 95112

Nomura Market
29583 Mission Blvd.
Hayward 94544

The Omodaka
115 Clement St.
San Francisco 94118

K. Sakai Co. (Uoki)
1656 Post St.
San Francisco 94115

Sanwa Market
2122 Cabrillo St.
San Francisco 94121

Suruki
140 Boothbay
Foster City 94404

Takahashi Company
221 S. Claremont St.
San Mateo 94401

SOUTHERN CALIFORNIA

Asahi Company
660 Oxnard Blvd.
Oxnard 93030

Ebisu Market
18940 Brookhurst St.
Fountain Valley 92708

Eiko Shoten
6082 University Ave.
San Diego 92115

Fujiya Market
601 N. Virgil Ave.
Los Angeles 90004

Fukuda's
2412 S. Escondido Blvd.
Escondido 92025

Motoyama Market
16135 S. Western Ave.
Gardena 90247

New Meiji Market
1620 W. Redondo Beach
Gardena 90247

Nippon Foods
2935 West Ball Rd.
Anaheim 92804

Omori's
2700 N. Santa Fe
Vista 92083

Sakae Oriental Grocery
4277 Convoy St.
San Diego 92111

S & N Food Market
2600 E. 1st Street
Los Angeles 90033

Senri Market
111 N. Lincoln Ave.
Monterey Park 91754

Yamamoto Bros
314 Wilmington Blvd.
Wilmington 90744

ILLINOIS

Diamond Trading Co.
913 W. Belmont Ave.
Chicago 60657

Furuya & Company
5358 N. Clark St.
Chicago 60640

Star Market
3349 N. Clark St.
Chicago 60657

NEW YORK

Harumi
318-320 W. 231 St.
Bronx 10463

Katagiri Company
224 East 59th St.
New York 10022

Meidiya
18 N. Central Park Ave.
Hartsdale 10530

Tanaka & Company
326 Amsterdam Ave.
New York 10023

Tokyo Sales Corp.
142 W. 57th St.
New York 10019

TEXAS

Edoya Oriental
223 Farmer Branch
Dallas 75234

Japanese Grocery
14366-B Memorial Dr.
Houston 77042

Nippon Daido Int'l
11138 Westheimer
Houston 77042

Tachibana
4886 Hercules Ave.
El Paso 79904

JAPANESE FOOD STORES IN CANADA

BRITISH COLUMBIA

Mihamaya
392 Powell St.
Vancouver B.C.

Shimizu Shoten
349 East Hasting St.
Vancouver B.C.

ONTARIO

Furuya Trading Co. Ltd.
460 Dundas St. West
Toronto
Ontario

Iwaki Japanese Food Store
2627 Yonge St.
Toronto
Ontario

Nakanishi Japan Food Store
465 Somerset St. West
Ottawa
Ontario

Sanko Trading Co.
221 Spandina Ave.
Toronta
Ontario

Yanagawa Japanese Foods
639 Upper James St.
Hamilton
Ontario

QUEBEC

Miyamoto Provisions
382 Victoria Ave.
Montreal Westmount
Quebec

Index

ACKNOWLEDGEMENTS

Restaurant Yamato
Charles Cosham
Reiko Sakuma
Michael Freeman
Japanese Tourist Office
Mick Hill
Mrs Kitanaka
Miss Murase
Mrs Sakamoto
Mr & Mrs Ishida
Mrs Terao